A Stornoway Life

from
Scotland Street *to* South Africa

D1514377

Readers may recognise the stories which, in an earlier version appeared in the author's popular column in 'Back in the Day' published by Stornoway Gazette.

First published in 2015 by Acair Ltd.

Reprinted in 2016 by Acair Ltd.,
An Tosgan
Seaforth Road
Stornoway
Isle of Lewis HS1 2SD

www.acairbooks.com
info@acairbooks.com

Cover photographs © Fiona Rennie

Book and Cover design by Margaret A. MacLeod

A CIP catalogue record for this title is available from the British Library

Printed and bound by Hussar Books, Poland

ISBN 978-086152-549-2

A
STORNOWAY
Life

from

Scotland Street *to* South Africa

Pat MacFarlane

This book is dedicated to the memory of our brother Alistair, who died at 12 years. Also to his friends Rory and Morris whose lives were short too.

Contents

Foreword

This memoir is absolutely fascinating. It is much more than a history of the town over the last two centuries. It is a treasure trove of personalities and of every day events melded with interesting descriptions of many of the best loved places in our town. It is also an eclectic but well observed and lovingly crafted account of the author's personal interaction with life as it was in his youth, his middle age and his present venerable stage of life. Through this charming and amusing memoir there is a subliminal description of that most enigmatic and entertaining of characters a "Stornoway Cove".

Peter "Pat" Macfarlane is himself one of the last of that almost extinct species of town worthies who until recently provided us with wit, wisdom and a highly individual expression of a view of life in the crucible and looking glass of community affairs. He is well known and affectionately regarded throughout the island he has adorned for more than ninety years.

At that time and indeed up until 1955 this area of town was a densely populated enclave, a village almost. Scores of children running riot in Scotland Street, dim gas lamp posts at each junction, many little shops (some even in the front room of the family home), and crowded back closes in which more than one family lived, behind the main house. It had Stornoway's only cinema, two blacksmith's, a hostelry (for horses), a dairy, the Fire Station and to end it all, a funeral undertaker's with horse drawn hearses. Moreover it was on the edge of the town's playgrounds, the harbour at the bottom of Spoil's Brae and the Castle Grounds. It is little wonder that such an intimate little community bred a race of people of independent personality, street wisdom and a keen sense of identity.

In the present days of centralised urban planning, we have our separate residential area, separate shopping area, separate playing area and separate entertainment area all "managed and limited" by so called Health and Safety Laws. Thus have we lost the real vibrancy of the community so beautifully described A Stornoway Life.

Our generation and more importantly, future generations are indebted to worthy citizens, so amply personified by Pat Macfarlane. His splendid memoir should be read with attention by town managers, for it will be treasured, not only by Stornowegians at home and abroad, but by all who desire the values of a good society.

Sandy Matheson
Alexander Matheson - Honorary President, Stornoway Historical Society

Introduction

This is not a traditional biography in the sense of a life followed on a chronological path. However, those of us who know the author will not be at all surprised that he has chosen an alternative route, opting instead to use a series of self-contained anecdotes and stories to reflect the times and tides in his long and remarkable life. Readers may recognise the stories which have originally appeared in his popular column in 'Back in the Day'; indeed, public interest in that column was one of the main reasons for Pat's decision to pull his tales together into a collection.

One constant in the stories, apart from Pat himself, is the house at 16 Scotland Street which has stood for the best part of two centuries and which has been his home for his entire ninety-plus years since his birth in August 1920, with the exception of his time in the RAF.

The house, its garden and outbuildings, feature prominently in the stories, helping to give the sense of place which I think is one of the strengths of Pat's tales. This sense of place extends to the immediate environs of Scotland Street, New Street, Keith Street and beyond to the town and island of the 1920s and 30s.

Balancing the local interest afforded by the opening three chapters, Chapter Four takes us quite literally to the other side of the world, with Pat's war experiences in South Africa and the Middle East. Having entered the services in 1938, Pat became a Sergeant in the RAF. The series of coincidences and amusing anecdotes which he shares here do not linger on the darker side of his war experiences, although he does hint at his increasing view of war as a futile exercise and a tragic waste of young lives.

His experiences on returning to Stornoway after the war are the subject matter of Chapter Five, taking us through a wide variety of businesses and other interests. Fittingly, one such interest is the island's past, with this volume making its own contribution to our shared knowledge of bygone times.

Many of the stories in this collection are the stories my sisters and I grew up listening to, particularly on Sunday afternoons and, almost always, at our own request. For us, the bare skeleton of the story was not the main event: what we wanted were the voices, the actions and the facial expressions of the characters involved; stories told so often that we knew not only the beginning, middle and ending, but all parts in between, demanding that the same formula was used at each telling.

We all had our favourites, brought to life memorably across the years by a skilled story teller. Some even became games: I vividly remember acting out the scene in the dressmaker's shop where my grandmother was engaged to learn to sew, with Pat playing the part of the exasperated employer facing his mutinous trainees. Whether the stories took us back to his own childhood or, even further back, to his mother's, we were entranced by the fact that the very house in which we were sitting was the backdrop to so many of the fabled events.

What comes through the pages of this book, first and foremost, is the author's capacity for life and laughter, and a huge generosity of spirit, manifested in many acts of kindness which he is far too modest to have detailed here.

Throughout his career as a Stornoway shop-keeper, Pat's physical presence in his businesses- from the grocery shop on Keith Street to 'Loch Erisort' on Cromwell Street- was key to their success. Customers returned again and again, drawn by his personality and the 'carry on' with the staff in the shops.

I hope that the essence of that personality is distilled here and that the publication of this volume will allow Pat's stories to bring pleasure to many readers in Stornoway and beyond.

Frances Murray

Stornoway

February 2015

Chapter 1

Where It All Began

The history of the house I live in, and the one next door, on Scotland Street is interesting, as are the various activities which went on in the yards behind them. The houses were built in the 1840s for two friends who were born in Melbost, near the present site of the airport.

One was John Gunn, who was a deep sea sailor making voyages to the Far East, and his friend's name was John Macrae who was a builder. John Macrae built both houses: No.14 for his family, and No.16 for John Gunn and his family. John Gunn was my great grandfather. There is a story that his wife, my great grandmother from Kintail, visited the site to inspect progress of the building as her husband was at sea at the time.

John Macrae was the builder of the sea wall from Cuddy Point to the mouth of the Creed, and the Porter's Lodge, the Free Church Manse (now no more), and several other well-known buildings. He built a second, smaller, house for himself at the rear of No.14. The idea was that the rent of the secondary buildings would pay the rates of the main one.

There are large yards behind both houses. John Macrae roofed over his entire yard, which was his builder's workshop; it is still there. John Gunn, being a seaman, did not make use of his yard, but the relatives from Melbost used to come to cut the grass to make hay.

A brother of John's, Alec, was also a seaman, and he decided to 'jump ship' and join the Gold Rush in South Australia. He got a licence, found a partner (which was a necessity) and off they went. Whaddayouknow! They found a nugget!

On the morning after the find, the partner said that he had spent most of the night praying because the Devil was tempting him to grab the nugget and run. He did not give in to temptation, and my great grand uncle, Alec Gunn, became a rich man and never came back to Lewis. Two of his sons went to English universities but never came to Stornoway. Sometimes, when I was short of cash, I used to daydream of an advert in 'The Gazette' from solicitors looking for relatives of Alec Gunn, late of Adelaide and Melbost. It didn't happen, and it's too late now.

The next development was that John Gunn, my great grandfather, decided to follow his brother's example and 'go for gold' too; he 'jumped ship' as well! You would have thought his brother would have given him a share of his new-found fortune so that he could have stayed at home. Sailors coming home from voyages reported seeing Alec Gunn driving through the streets of Adelaide in some kind of horse-drawn vehicle, looking prosperous - possibly an exaggeration.

Anyway, John decided not to trust 'pardners' and went panning with some kind of a sieve. I don't know if this was done in a river or a kind of gravel pit, but he apparently did get some returns from his work, and dutifully sent his gains home to his wife.

Eventually he retired from sea-going, at least from long voyages. It was said that although he was not qualified as a skipper (and apparently formal papers were not always required) he was able to sail smaller craft, delivering cargoes, possibly cured or dried fish, to Continental ports.

My grandfather, their son Peter, was born at 16 Scotland Street in 1850. When he grew up and 'graduated' as a blacksmith, he started a business for himself in the yard behind No. 16. He cobbled over the yard (still to be seen) and built stables along two sides with stables for 20 horses. This was for overnight accommodation for horses after long journeys into town - B&B for horses. The fee was 9d which went up to 1 shilling (or 5p in today's money) if they stayed after 11 p.m.

A practical joke was played on my mother when she was running the stables. At that time there was an article called a hat stand in the lobby. It had several biggish hooks on it and a glove drawer in the middle. (I never saw gloves in it.) One of the conspirators on this occasion sneaked in to the lobby and quietly took away my mother's cloak and a large hat and, unknown to her, untied a horse and mounted it. Wearing the cloak and hat, he rode off away up Keith Street. My mother had heard a horse going out but, as she didn't see anyone, she assumed it was one of the customers sneaking off to dodge the fee—money was scarce then.

Then off the rider galloped with the hat pulled down over his face and the cloak covering his body, up and down the streets. The other brother and co-conspirator came along, pretending to try to stop it. People started coming out of their houses, and the brother running along shouted, "That's Kate! We were just having a laugh, showing her how to sit on the horse and it bolted. Try to catch the reins!"

At last, when both horse and rider were probably tired, they came back to where they had started. My mother came out of the house and someone shouted, "Kate, was that not you on the horse?"

"What do you mean?" she said. "Me, on a horse?"

The rider then jumped off and gave her back her cloak and hat. "Oh, you demon!" she said, realising that the Macrae brothers had played a good trick and that everyone had enjoyed a good laugh.

Peter Gunn built a smiddy with a forge, anvils, and whatever other tools were required for the trade. He made fire-irons, shod horses, made stamps for impressing identification marks on sheep's horns, and so on. He employed a joiner to make the wooden part of cartwheels while he made the iron rim. This was heated in an outside fire pit until it was red-hot, then applied to the wheel and dowsed with water, making it contract onto the wheel.

With the builder's yard next door and my grandfather's activities it was a busy and noisy area, over a period of about 40 years. After his death, the premises were let to various people; I think the late Ossian Macaskill was there for a while. Another temporary tenant was a group of cattle buyers from Easter Ross known as the 'Brecans' who mostly bought calves, and used one of our stables as a place to keep them while they went round collecting others.

Watching these young animals being hustled out a vehicle and shoved into a shed aroused my sympathy. I thought they were crying for their mothers, but it was probably for a drink of milk as much as anything. I remember wondering if I could sneak round and open the door to let them out at night. Of course, it would have been just as disastrous for them to be wandering around the town when their home was probably in Uig or Ness. Besides, the 'Brecans' were staying in a B&B across the road.

Another time they came they were collecting turkeys, and again they rented a stable to keep them in while gathering more. I stood watching the performance. The turkeys were not pleased as they were manhandled from one place to another. One of the 'Brecans' called to me, "Hey, wee fellow, you stand at the close in case one gets away, and don't let any out!" So I stood, hoping none would escape. Suddenly, a huge, angry turkey, almost as big as myself, came bounding out! I was certainly scared, and, although I didn't exactly wave it on, I stood aside, and it galloped down Scotland Street. I don't know why, maybe to make the 'Brecans' think I had tried to stop it, but I ran after it, down the Kenneth Street brae, across Bayhead and onto the quay. There were fishing boats there, and another bigger boat with a mast and rigging was at the quayside.

The turkey stood, considering its options, and chose the big boat. It flapped and scrambled its way up the mast with difficulty, through the rigging to where it obviously thought it was safe. That bird was trying to save its life. Just then, the 'Brecans' appeared on Bayhead and saw me on the quay. "Where did it go?" one demanded. To my shame, I pointed up the mast, and they started shouting rude things at the turkey.

"Come down here, you so-and-so!"

The turkey answered in 'gobbledegook' (or turkey language), "Not on your life." Each side then considered what to do. The turkey was quiet. I imagined it was thinking to itself, "I haven't a chance here, and Christmas is coming." Suddenly, it leapt off the 'spiris' and flapped (they don't fly very well) down into the sea.

It disappeared among the fishing boats. I always hoped it had made it to the Castle Grounds and lived happily ever after. Our gang spent a lot of time in the Grounds but we never saw it. Somehow I felt that I had let that bird down, and I think of it every Christmas when I'm carving.

Over the next few years, the premises were mostly empty. Gradually, as horses were replaced by cars, the stables were no longer needed, so they were good places in which to play.

A later animal-related story happened when I was would have been at least eleven years old, and remarkably ignorant. I was sitting beside Geordie Pordie (Willie Bucach's brother) in school and one day he asked me, "Do you want to buy a rabbit?" I hadn't thought of it but said yes and made a hutch out of a barrel. Geordie arrived with a huge rabbit, mostly white.

He said, "It's a 'she' and," poking her middle, "I think she's going to have young ones. You will know if you see her pulling the fur off her chest and making a nest," which indeed she did.

One day I peeped into the nest and there was a heap of tiny, blind, naked rabbits. Of course, they grew up quickly and were soon running all over the yard.

Geordie said, "You can sell them for 9d each," which I did.

After that batch was sold, I asked Geordie when the rabbit would have another lot.

"Oh, you'll need a 'he' for that," he said.

"What for?" I quizzed.

He just looked at me. "I'll take mine down," he said. So, down he came with a huge 'he'. It was obvious they had met before and 'she' didn't like him. There was quite an audience of local children. "Why are they fighting?" I heard one say.

Soon Geordie came back for his 'he' and, in due course, 'she' started pulling fur off her chest, and soon the yard was covered in black and white rabbits again, and I became quite rich like my great grand uncle Alec in Adelaide! I don't remember how this poor rabbit escaped in the end and the rabbit trade ended. There was a short spell with white mice too- very unpopular with certain grown-ups. I remember one being taken to school in somebody's pocket and released. Every girl in the class, including the lady teacher, was up on top of her desk, screaming. Actually, this may have been a wild, grey mouse that we had caught in a trap.

Recently, I met 'Byshie' (married to the late Joan Mackenzie, a one-time Mod medallist). He told me that he had once bought a rabbit from me for 9d. I thought he had a complaint and wanted his money back. "Have you still got it?" I asked.

"Rabbits don't live for nearly a century!" was his reply.

I remember many funny incidents from my own past, but it is more difficult now to remember the stories I heard from older generations when I was young myself. One lady who came home every year as long as she could and liked to talk about her youth was Lena Montgomery. She, it was, who recounted the story about the day a floor collapsed and a barrel of salt herring fell down into the bed of a woman who lived below. At that time, because Kenneth Street and Cromwell Street are on different levels, a room on Cromwell Street was occupied by a solitary lady, and, on the level above, there was a butcher's shop with its entrance on Kenneth Street. It was the custom then for small food shops to sell salt herring from a barrel which was always rolled out onto the pavement during the hours of business and rolled back in at night.

The herring was in brine, which, being salty, preserved the fish. Very likely, it also caused a certain dampness under the barrel, which always stood in the same place in the shop. One terrible day there was a loud crack as the floorboards underneath the barrel gave way, and it, and its smelly contents, fell through the floor into the women's bed, which, as usual in those days, had curtains round it. Fortunately, the woman was not in the bed, or it might have been curtains for her too!

She was in the room, so, when she got her breath back, she started shouting up at the hole in the ceiling, "You stupid so-and-so! Wait 'til I get a hold of your neck!"

Then the curtains round the bed moved, and the butcher's voice said, "You don't need to wait; I'm here too!" He had been standing beside the barrel. There was always so much laughter in the telling of this story that I never heard the final outcome.

The Castle Grounds as they were in Lena's youth, probably in the 1890s, had been in existence for about 50 years by this time and were at their best; well maintained and supervised by professional gardeners and rangers (or 'watchers' as we called them in our time). The public needed a pass, obtained from the Estate Office, to get in. The area around the Castle was called the Private Gardens and was especially well looked after. The paths through the flower-beds and bushes were lined with flowers. In the spring there were different colours of primroses. Entry to the magnificent glasshouses was only allowed along with an adult. (I remember being in at least once.) There was a fish pond with a fountain. It was forbidden to pick flowers, but one day, Lena and her friend decided to take the risk, concealing two small posies of primroses in their blouses.

Going past the Porter's Lodge, trying to look innocent, Lena felt something moving in her blouse, and then a buzzing inside as well. Terrified as she was of bees, she was even more terrified of the Watcher inside. She managed to keep going until she was out of his sight before the screaming and thumping started!

In my time things were different: there was no-one living in the Porter's Lodge and there were several entrances to the Grounds. They were still watched by two gentlemen who walked the paths continuously. Our crowd was not destructive. We were interested in identifying the various birds and watching their nests and climbing quite high trees. Sandy Flett was one of gang, and his grandparents were caretakers, living in the Castle, and likely a good influence.

In terms of the Grounds, an unfortunate mistake was made. Someone introduced Rhododendron Ponticum and Salmon Berry, both very invasive species which are banned in most other similar estates, including Inverewe. Large areas of the Castle Grounds have ben choked by these two bushes. Changes of ownership, shortage of cash and two World Wars all contributed to a period of neglect.

Another of Lena's stories was about a day she and others were playing with a ball in the street when it went over one of the famous Stornoway

17

railings. They decided to creep in the back gate to rescue the ball but it was locked. So over they went, probably enjoying the danger. Whether true or not, they had decided the householder was a bit of a tiger as far as 'street urchins' were concerned. Suddenly, one said, "Here's the man! Let's go!" The gang managed to scramble over the gate, all except my mother. At that time it was the fashion for girls to wear a sash wrapped around the waist. Her sash got hooked on one of the spikes of the gate, so she hung there until the householder arrived. There was nothing he could do but lift her down, and probably tell them to "clear away to their own quarters!" This was a familiar phrase to be shouted by householders afraid of broken windows.

Another story involved the rowing boats that were always casually moored near the steps at the end of the Inner Harbour, oars not removed or locked. The owners did not seem to mind small people going out for a row. A mixed group, boys and girls, set off to row to Arnish. When they were well out in the harbour they realised they were 'taking in water'. There was great panic. The bung had come out and they could not find it!

They altered course for the shore, the boys rowing like mad and the girls baling out as fast as they could with the boys' caps. It could have been a tragedy as none of them could swim. They made it to the mouth of the Creed just in time and left the boat, about to sink, climbed up the rocks and got home through the Grounds. I presume the owner managed to retrieve the boat later!

On the subject of personalities in the period before the First War, I remember a shop in Stornoway called The Baltic Bootshop. It was owned, strangely, by a man from one of the Baltic countries, called Bitner. I don't think he was resident in Stornoway, or even whether he ever visited. He employed a series of local ladies over the years. One, Annie, was in charge for many years, earning the title 'Annie the Bootshop'. Before her time, I think, there was a lady called Zamma, who was quite a personality and, from memory of her later visits to my mother, very pretty.

The shop became a favourite meeting place for some of the young people of the town, mostly girls. From hearing their recollections I got the impression that if a fisherman or a crofter came in to buy a pair of boots he was looked on as a nuisance for interrupting their party. However, the fishing industry, in particular herring, brought many men from outside the island here on business. A few must have landed up in the Bootshop because I know of a few marriages which started there. Zamma herself was one who married and went to live in the Isle of Wight, to the disappointment of her friends.

Another of the group, Janet, who was a bit of rebel and had an eye-catching style of dress, was a real entertainer at the parties in the Bootshop. She, too, left the island for marriage to a farmer on the mainland. The story I used to hear about her was that, some time after her departure, when the rest of the group was gathered for their afternoon meeting, who swept in but the lady in question.

"Janet!" they all yelled. "Where did you come from?"

Janet took her hat off, threw it on the counter, sat on a box and said, "That's it. I came home last night and I'm not going back. ME- milk a cow? No fear- I'm terrified of them!"

She then entertained her friends (probably with a little exaggeration) with stories about what she was expected to do on the farmyard. Suddenly, in the middle of all the yarns and laughter, the figure of a man appeared in the doorway. He just said one word – "Janet" – and crooked his finger at her. There was silence. Then she put out her cigarette, picked up her hat, and off she went with him, quiet as a mouse.

I don't know how long it was before she started coming again on holiday, but she did stay on the farm and bring up a family there. One day, many years later, I was working at the back of the house and came inside for something. Before I reached the living room I heard the gales of laughter. Peeping in, I saw two white heads and an elderly hand in the air holding a cigarette. At first glance I thought it was my mother. "Has she gone mad?" I was thinking. "She hates smoking!" Soon I realised it was the other lady, and, as they were obviously enjoying reminiscing, I did not intrude. I found out later that the visitor was the rebel Janet. While she was at home on holiday she stayed with her sister-in-law who didn't approve of ladies smoking, so she went round those of her friends who allowed smoking, including, at this time, our house. Not today, though!

During the War, I met friends of a Macdonald family in Johannesburg whom I will mention later. Mr Macdonald had a brother, Murdo, who had an interesting career in Stornoway which my mother used to tell me about. It had come to the attention of the inhabitants of the Castle, the Mathesons, that Murdo was very talented at making clothes. They arranged for him to go to London and then Paris to learn more about these arts. Eventually, he came back to the town where he set up an 'Haute Couture' salon.

From having seen musicals in London, he learned how to imitate the male stars of the time and performed at concerts in the Town Hall. He was somewhat pear-shaped, and dressed up in tails, silk scarves, white gloves and black tie. He sauntered around the stage singing the popular songs of the town such as 'The Man Who Broke the Bank in Monte Carlo' and 'Burlington Bertie from Bow'. It seems he was a great success, both on the stage and in the salon. It was quite an achievement to be able to afford an outfit made by Murdo.

When he got an order to make a whole trousseau, he would wash the whole salon and scrub the floor before opening the rolls of velvet and satin. At one time my mother and two friends (Isabella Morrison, later Mrs Whittaker and Murdina Montgomery who became Mrs Percy Young) were engaged by him to learn to sew. He got a trousseau order and told the girls to scrub the floor as was his custom.

"What?" they said. "We didn't come here to scrub floors. No fear."

"You impudent upstarts," he shouted. "Who do you think you are?"

They still refused, so he got a pail of hot water, a scrubbing brush and scouring cloth, and started scrubbing, all the time giving them a tongue lashing as he was well able to do. The girls wore long skirts then, and as one of them was passing him by, her skirt caught on the pail, tipping water over his trousers as he scrubbed. He flew into a frenzy of rage and accused my mother of having done it deliberately. He picked up the wet scouring cloth and went for her. There was no time to explain that it had been an accident, and that she had not been responsible in any case, so she fled downstairs and along Bayhead with Murdo after her.

There were many tailors in Stornoway at that time, many of them disabled and doing their work sitting down. My mother dived into the first tailor's shop she came to and took refuge behind the tailor. When Murdo came in, the tailor raised a restraining hand and urged him to calm down. I assume peace was restored.

He attended the Episcopalian Church. At one time, the Bishop was in town on an official visit and the Rector took him to see Murdo. A neighbour called Katie de Litus (her father was foreign) answered the door and went up to tell Murdo about his visitors. Murdo was in his shirt and braces. He was panic-stricken about not being properly dressed.

"Tell them I'm not in," he ordered Katie, so she went down and said politely, "I'm sorry. Mr Macdonald seems to have gone out."

In the meantime, Murdo was leaning over the bannister, out of sight, listening to the conversation below. Suddenly the bannister cracked and broke under his weight, and he rolled down the stairs, landing at the clerics' feet. He rounded on Katie. "What do you mean, Katie de Litus, telling these gentlemen that I wasn't in?"

After the churchmen left, Katie gave him what for!

He used to have afternoon tea-parties for his best customers for which he would use his silver tea service. One day, as the ladies were waiting for their tea, Murdo appeared from the kitchen and said, "I'm sorry ladies, the party is b*******. The arse fell out of the teapot!" Obviously he forgot that you don't put silver teapots onto a hotplate!

He once sent my mother to Roddy Smith's for a packet of De Reske cigarettes, saying he would call to pay for them himself. The lady in the shop smiled sweetly and said, "Oh, yes. Well just tell Mr Macdonald he can have the cigarettes when he pays for the last lot!"

More rage from Murdo when this was reported to him: "Did she say that, the so-and-so?"

It seems that even on his death-bed, he couldn't resist the spiky remark. Some friends and clients were visiting, taking a last look at their sparring partner. He was getting weaker and someone was trying to give him a teaspoon of whisky.

"Oh, no, poor Murdo can't take it," he said. But," he whispered, pointing at one of the ladies, "give it to Maggie... she's very fond of it."

I mentioned Percy Young earlier. His father was a salmon exporter and they lived in Sandwick. (I think there is a still a model of a salmon displayed on the outside wall of the house.) This was in the days before refrigeration and they had an ingenious method of obtaining ice to pack in the fish boxes for transport to the mainland. They made a room which was dug out into a bank and built up so it had extra thick walls, no windows and, I suppose, a very tightly shutting door. An artificial pond was constructed and filled with water. It froze in the winter. When it was well frozen over, a horse was persuaded to walk over it. The broken ice was then packed into boxes and stored in the special 'ice house'. Being kept away from air, the ice did not melt and was available for sending away fish in the season.

The pond was also used by children for skating. It was only a few inches deep so it was not dangerous and, as far as I know, the Youngs did not seem to mind. The ice house was not a novel invention: there was another one, close to the Castle, near the Shoe Burn, which probably supplied the ice for their needs. I believe it was usual for large estate houses to have one.

On the subject of the Shoe Burn, I wonder if the origins of its name are well known now? In earlier times, people making their way to town from the Lochs district usually walked barefoot. When they reached the burn, they washed their feet and put on their shoes which they had been carrying. Then they proceeded into town to do their business. Hence the Shoe Burn or Allt na Brog.

Such were the tales of Stornoway 120 years ago that I often heard repeated.

Cromwell Street, early 20th century.

Pat's grandfather, Peter Gunn, the Blacksmith (right) with his apprentice.

16 Scotland Street - and Pat today.

Chapter 2

Games and Ploys of the 20s and 30s

Looking back on the days of my youth, especially from this same house where I have always stayed, with the exception of six years of enforced absence (not the jail!), gives me the feeling that I am living now in the dim and distant future, and the past is where I really belong.

I wonder if anyone else remembers the two tourist ships that used to come to Stornoway's No. 1 Pier in the 1920s or 30s, called *The Killarney* and *The Lady Killarney*? Or maybe it was the same ship with a slight change of name?

At that time, the quays (and under the quays) were favourite playgrounds, especially for boys. A memorable event was the annual arrival of these two ships, and their departure. Pocket money was quite hard to come by for most of us, and we needed money for a lot of our activities: visits to Archie Crae's shop; JS Macleans; and Finlay's on Church Street; and getting into the matinee in Will Mack's picture house.

So, when The Killarney was leaving and the passengers threw 'largesse' onto the quay it was very welcome, even although it was mostly brown coins. One day, though, what did I spy but a big white coin, all by itself- a half-crown no less! With mounting excitement, I bent down to pick it up…and a big tackety boot landed on the back of my hand. I looked up to see a 'big guy'; I knew him by sight- he was a little older and spent his time around the harbour and the fishing boats and was a bit of a character. I didn't feel inclined to argue, so I said goodbye to 'my' first half-crown- an introduction to the harsh facts of life. The owner of the tackety boot became a much-admired hero later on.

On the theme of disappointments, another incident on the quay comes back to me. About this time there was a gentleman in business in the island who was the only Jew, as far as I know, to do this. His name was Alexander Kravitch, but the 'locals' changed this to Alasdair Mor. He was quite popular because he had the typical humour and repartee of the Jewish folk. Although he had a shop for a time on the main street near to the junction of Bayhead and Cromwell Street, one day he set up a stall opposite the foot of Church Street, probably to stimulate a little more trade, being in the centre of the town.

On the stall there was the usual display of odds and ends. There was a group of fellows, much older than me, but still young, round the stall, listening to Alasdair's sales talk and having a few laughs back and fore. I was only little and just listened and watched. I don't remember seeing anyone buying anything. Probably no-one had any money; I know I hadn't.

Alasdair held up a wrist watch which was something I had a great longing for.

"Who'll buy a watch?" asked Alasdair. "Just ten shillings." Much laughter. "Alright. Eight shillings, anybody?" Plenty laughs but no takers. So it came down, shilling by shilling. At last, "Who'll take it for nothing?" came from Alasdair Mor. More laughs, but my heart lurched and up went my hand. Then came the gales of laughter, and back into the box went the watch.

I suppose I ran away, feeling embarrassed at having been such a clown, but I was only little! Maybe another lesson?

The main difference between then and now is that in the 20s and 30s this part of Scotland Street and Keith Street were very lively places. Now the area is deadly quiet. We had a builder's yard where we played, two smiddies, a dairy, a small laundry and a garage. We used to be able to at least visit these places without being thrown out. In the garage there was a pre-First World War vintage car. I wonder what happened to it and what it would be worth today?

The dairy was a model of efficiency and cleanliness. The noise of the milk cans being delivered from the farms and the empties being taken away and duly washed and sterilised caused a stir twice daily.

Ladies who came to buy milk, cream, skimmed milk, butter, buttermilk, crowdie and sometimes cheese, made the area lively and cheerful.

Next to the dairy was a store selling feed stuff for the animals. This was delivered through a gap in the wall straight onto the lorry or cart of the customer. One sad day a cart and horse were standing awaiting the load coming out when, suddenly, something happened to the horse; maybe she was stung by a cleg.

She took off and galloped down Scotland Street and went halfway through the window of what is now Clendy's house. A family sitting at their table were suddenly joined by half a horse. Children round about were told that she refused to come near Scotland Street any more, but we were not so naïve to believe that: we knew she had met her watery grave at the Cockle Ebb. She had been the only horse in Tolsta Chaolais and was much missed.

The dairy and the grain store were managed by Mr Murdo Smith, father of Ian Smith, a well-known singer and grandfather of Margaret Maciver. Sometimes, local boys were given baskets of butter and crowdie to go round the town selling them. We were told that if we heard the people speaking Gaelic we had to say "An ceannaich sibh gruth no im?" We would then get a few pennies to help us get into the pictures.

Near the dairy was a small private laundry run by two elderly women from Aberdeenshire and a younger assistant from Carloway. The two women had retired from service in the Castle and they worked until their nineties, getting up at five or six every morning to light the boiler.

Mary, the assistant, whose fiancé was lost on the Iolaire, was quiet and sad, but she practically adopted me and even used to take me on holiday with her to Carloway. I seemed to spend a lot of time between the dairy and the laundry and, unfortunately, one day I did something to which I must confess.

Bella Morison who lived round the corner on Keith Street called to me, "Hi boy, do you know how to take a mouse out of a trap?" I think I was very young, not yet in school, and I had probably never seen a mouse before – dead or alive - and was certainly too young to have any anti-mouse feelings. She gave me a small 'goody' bag into which I would deposit the creature. Deed done, and on the spur of the moment, I decided to play a little trick on Maggie (the Dairy). Offering her the bag, I asked, "Would you like a goody, Maggie?"

"Oh, what a kind little boy. Thank you very much," she exclaimed. I didn't expect the shrieks and hysteria which followed and, as I took off, all I could hear was her yelling, "You horrible little boy!"

I'm sorry, now, Maggie.

Duncan 'The Major' Morison lived upstairs in part of the Seminary and sometimes the sound of music floated down from his music room. However, the centre of our lives was the 'Picture House' which had its entrance on Keith Street, and was next to the dairy, the laundry and the Seminary. It was run by Will Mack, a small man who was a little like Charlie Chaplin in some ways, and who was helped by the two Macgregor sisters, Gladys and Greta.

At night this was the centre of the town: the bright light of the Picture House, the stir of the night's entertainment. Sometimes Will walked up and down on the pavement announcing the programme: "Two reels Bobby Dunn and two reels Tom Mix!" (which were cowboy films) and then, of course, the big picture.

Two sweetie shops were open late: Archie's, directly opposite the Picture House, and John 'S' Maclean's, opposite Murray's Garage.

Besides the silent black and white films, the Picture House sometimes put on stage productions. Will Mack did a song and dance routine; Gladys, who seemed to be the younger sister and had bobbed hair, did some dancing and sang modern songs ('K-K-K-Katie in the C-C-C-Cowshed'); Greta, who was more perchink and had ringlets, sang songs such as 'Come into the garden, Maud.'

They sometimes taught local children to do sketches and 'turns'. I remember Al Crae sitting on the stage playing a tune on one of his father, the undertaker's, saws.

Another sketch involved Margaret I. (Tully) playing a fairy or an angel. She had to trip about the stage smiling whilst a crescent moon descended. She was to recline on the moon (there was a little seat at the back), and then be transported into the air behind the curtain. 'Splinjy', who lived next door to us, was engaged to operate this rope *trick*. Coming down was fine, but Margaret was not built for flying up on a moon. From the cheap seats in the front we could hear the gasping of 'Splinjy' in the wings, trying to haul Margaret up, but he could only manage to get her about a foot off the floor.

Her angelic expression changed to fury as she hung onto the moon's horns, glaring at poor 'Splinjy', before exiting stage left.

On one occasion, a group of older boys was playing a game that involved throwing stones onto the corrugated iron roof of the Picture House. I don't think it was intended to annoy anyone- just to see if they could manage it. Ishbel Kennedy's youngest brother, Donnie, was my friend at the time. As we had probably been told to 'clear off', we just watched. Suddenly, Will Mack appeared, wielding an axe. Of course, the big fellows scarpered, but we didn't move - we were, after all, innocent. Anyway, when we saw him coming in our direction, we thought this was no time for explanations, so we took off straight across the street into my house, and slammed the door, desperately trying to turn the key which was never used.

Just in time we locked the door, but then heard Will's footsteps going round the back of the house, so we dashed to lock the back door as well. We went up to the staircase window from where we saw Will Mack, still wielding the axe, looking into every shed. For the rest of Donnie's life, he and I wondered if Will would have scalped us if he had caught us that day!

Learning how unjust life can be in this situation reminds me of when Miss Read gave me the strap only an hour into my first day at school. My crime? I had only been watching older boys climbing a forbidden tree. I didn't know what her intention was when she said, "Put out your hands!" Maybe I thought she wanted to shake hands, as I had been taught! Anyway, I've forgiven you now, Miss Read, wherever you are!

I have another memory from the Picture House; there was a girl called Ooni Ullapool (don't ask me why!) who was engaged to play suitable music on the piano in relation to what was happening on the screen during the silent films. On one occasion, Ooni couldn't have been watching closely enough. She saw sea and ships, but couldn't have noticed the sailors desperately clinging to the wreckage of *The Birkenhead*. She plonked out the jolly tune, 'A Life on the Ocean Wave'.

Maybe it was after that that Duncan Morison (Major) got the job at 7/6d a week. He could compose tunes on the spot. He had different tunes for the Indians who rode bareback and bounced around, to the cowboys or Mounties who had saddles and had a slower movement.

Stornoway boys could earn a few pennies in different ways. We always carried bits of string in our pockets because when the herring boats were swinging across to the quay some of the fish would slip off the full baskets. A fight would follow between small boys and seagulls to grab the fallen ones. You could get a shilling for twenty 'skeds'. Some children at the other end of the town (Newton and Inaclete Road) made kipper boxes, but Scotland Street was too far from the kippering areas for us to do that.

Occasionally we earned some money by selling empty jam jars or bottles back to the shops. If you sold about a dozen 'Gazettes' you could earn a few pennies.

A woman in Bayhead once called me to go round the houses selling small bunches of flowers out of her garden for 3d each. I sold them quickly because they were nice and cheap and received a few pennies commission. I must have been very young because I didn't object to this; I would have been too embarrassed if I had been older!

There were a lot of children round Scotland Street and Keith Street. Down from us were the Nicholsons (3); further up, the Afrins (hundreds!);

ourselves (3); the Scotland Street part of the Seminary (2); Iain Beag and his brothers (6); Splinjys (5); further up, the Campbells (7 or 8) and the Tullys (3).

On Keith Street there were two Maclean families. On one side John S's four girls, one of them, Muriel, widow of Kenneth still living in the town, and her sister Joan lives in Canada. Across the road were Johnny, who became Assistant Post Master, Nessie, Morag and Anna. Murdo emigrated very young and we didn't know him. (Anna is the mother of former Chancellor of the Exchequer, Alistair Darling.) Jackie and Bunty Macleod lived next door. (Bunty's husband was later Auditor General and Accountant General in the Central African Federation, the two Rhodesias and Malawi.)

Joan Maclean liked to play football with the boys. Sometimes they said no, so she would go into her father's shop (John S's) and 'acquire' a few sweets to bribe the boys to let her be the goalie. Being tall she was quite good in goal, but she gave it up to become a nurse!

At the top end of Scotland Street there were big villa type houses, but children were very scarce there.

We played a variety of street games as the street is very broad and there was very little traffic. Some of the ditties for choosing teams had strange words. One that was used in my mother's childhood in the 1880s was, "Enicom, denicom, figum, fogum, benicom, nogum, severa, bevera, boof." This was condensed in our time to, "En, den, fi, fo, ben, no, se, be, boof." What ancient language did this come from, I wonder?

When the days started getting darker, about October, Calum the lamplighter came round, and there seemed to be a special atmosphere on the streets, especially if there was good weather at Hallowe'en. The most exciting game at this time was called 'Scout'. Two teams were chosen: one stayed in the den (under the lamp on the Seminary corner) and counted to a hundred, then went to look for the other team who could hide in the area between Keith Street, New Street, Bayhead and Scotland Street. It could be very dark, garden walls had to be climbed and old sheds had to be found to hide in. One good hiding place was a loft above Jimmy Afrin's stables in a lane behind Bayhead. It was cosy and warm in there, full of hay, with the polished horses down below giving off some warmth. We had to keep very quiet up there, especially when the others came into search for us. A twig could be heard snapping.

If you were discovered, you had to escape and run like mad back to the den, closely followed by the hunters of course. Soon after playing these games, we were swallowed up by the madness of war games. It's a short step from twelve to eighteen years of age. Two of the people I knew then didn't make it back from Dunkirk- John Campbell from Scotland Street (one of the Kylers) and Neillie Dan Macaulay who had worked in the dairy.

Thinking now about all the games and activities we took part in as children, it is amazing what long periods of time we spent wandering and no-one seemed to worry. Once a few of us went in a 'borrowed' rowing boat to Arnish, with some picnic things that Sandy Flett's Auntie Mary Ann gave us, and we didn't mention this to any of our parents. This was the only time there were search parties looking for us because we were gone for hours.

Besides the street games we freely roamed the Castle Grounds, finding birds' nests to watch until the young ones flew, and climbing trees in what we thought was a 'Tarzan' manner. There were a few scary experiences. Donnie Murray from New Street once decided to pass from one tree to another quite high up, by walking along a branch and holding on to the one above his head. Of course, as the branches got thinner, they bent down. At last he was stretched between two branches about halfway up, and could not move. I was down below, wondering what on earth to do, when Donnie suddenly shouted, "I'm coming down!" He let go, and although he crashed into other branches on the way down which helped to break his fall, he still hit the ground hard. He was completely winded, purple in the face and unable to speak or breathe. I didn't know what to do and felt like running back to the town to get help, but Donnie grabbed my arm and indicated that I should thump his back, which I did repeatedly, and eventually he recovered. That was a scary moment.

I had a disagreeable experience after that which seemed to be a kind of judgement which I deserved. I gave an account of Donnie's fall (with graphic descriptions, sound effects and desperate hand gestures) to the pals who had not been there. It became my star turn for a while and gave the gang many laughs. Then, one day, a horsebox was standing empty on the quay. It was simply a box with two sides joined by two high rungs on top, and with opening doors at the ends. It was used to escort horses off the boats (they weren't allowed to walk down the gangway with the other passengers). Our gang members were trying to make a circus act by swinging on one rung, letting go and catching hold of the other rung as we flew out the other end of the box. Of course, I missed and fell back onto the base of the box. It didn't seem painful, but when I stood up, I realised I wasn't breathing. I started producing groaning sounds and desperate appeals for someone to thump my back.

Unfortunately, the others thought I was doing my usual act, imitating Donnie, and they just stood, laughing. Along came a slightly older chap, Alex Jappy, who seemed to sense the seriousness of the situation and knew what to do. I'm not surprised that Alex reached a high rank in the Police. He made me walk and raise my arms above my head which apparently opens your lungs – what a relief! I don't think I ever thanked Alex, and now it's too late.

But, if any of you ever get winded, whether falling from a tree or out of a horse box, raise your arms above your head; it worked for me!

I had my own moment of fear up a tree in the Castle Grounds. We had heard that some hooded crows and ravens attacked sheep and newborn lambs, pecking their eyes out. On the harbour side of Gallows Hill there was a group of very tall, about 50 foot, pine trees that had nests at the top. Sandy Flett, the Murray twins and I, thinking these were the 'bad' crows' nests, decided we would climb up and remove some of the eggs so that there would be fewer of them to attack the sheep and lambs.

The twins were small and light and seemed to swarm up the trees like monkeys. I don't recollect whether or not they managed to get any eggs, but of course I had to follow suit. With great difficulty, I forced my way through the scratchy pine needles until I was right under the nests. These were made of twigs and were added to every year so that they were actually like an enormous platform about two feet deep. I couldn't even think of letting go one arm to stretch round the nest for the eggs, and the branch I was clinging to was thin and prickly. A wind had got up; with my weight and the weight of the nests the tree tops began to sway alarmingly, giving me tantalising glimpses across the harbour of the town, which I thought I would never walk in again. I was being dive-bombed by screeching, angry black birds, protecting their eggs.... Coming down was worse as I could see the furious face of Goosey, the Watcher, at the bottom looking up at me, waiting to give me a row. We weren't supposed to be climbing trees at all, but I was very glad to get back on firm ground.

Between the town streets, the Castle Grounds and the harbour, our playing area was pretty big. As I mentioned earlier, rowing boat owners tended to leave their boats tied in Bayhead with the oars left in them, perhaps expecting small boys to 'borrow' them as long as they stayed in the inner harbour. I had been looking forward to seeing a carnival in the town on one occasion, but my companions were scornful of this event and persuaded me to go for a row instead. We proceeded into the outer harbour; it was a bit rough but manageable as long as we were near the shore. Suddenly, however, we found ourselves in open water facing really big waves. We knew enough about boats to realise that we would be swamped if we tried to turn.

There were some old boats permanently anchored near the lighthouse and used as 'coalers' for coal burning ships. They were known as 'the hulks'. Workers going home from these hulks in their own boat spotted our plight and were waving and shouting warnings. One of our crew, probably Angie Crockett with his family background of boats and lifeboat, shouted, "Make for the hulks!" This we did, and managed to turn in the lee of one of them. It's a wonder no-one sent out the lifeboat as, when we reached the quay, there was quite a crowd watching the drama, possibly including the owner of the boat.

There was another quayside episode in the 'Tarzan' mode. The Murray twins, Kya and Doy, saw a tempting rope looping down from the quay and up to the prow of a fishing boat at high tide. One after the other, they proceeded along the rope, hand over hand, and boarded the boat. With some trepidation, I followed them. I made it to the lowest point of the rope but, too late, I couldn't climb up. I just dangled there, being gaped at by my pals on the quay. Being unable to move in either direction along the rope, eventually I just let go.

I went straight down, through the dark, dirty water into the mud at the bottom. I came up gasping and managed somehow to thrash my way over to the quay wall where there happened to be a handy iron ladder. Before I reached the ladder, I heard a certain party shouting, "Save my brother!" (He has always denied this since.) I trudged home, smelling and looking anything but nice.

There were encounters between gangs from various parts of the town which seemed scary at the time, but, looking back, were probably mostly 'pretend'. Once I saw the 'Kenneth Streets' coming down to where we had arranged to meet them in a field at Mackenzie Street, armed with the usual brushes, planks and clothes poles. What was a bit alarming was that there was a guy at the back carrying a box marked with a red cross… I don't remember anyone being whacked with a clothes pole, however.

One summer, when I was eight or nine years old, I had a strange holiday. I remember clearly making a big fuss at home because other boys I knew were going away for their summer holidays on the boat, with the possibility of seeing trains and double decker buses on the mainland. I think I must have been an obnoxious child because, amazingly, they gave in to me. There was an aunt and her husband in Montrose whom I had never seen; in desperation, my parents arranged to parcel me up and send me to them. They had no children and actually offered to keep me and send me to a local fee-paying school. He was a retired businessman and had been a Sergeant Major in the First World War. (I later came across others of this type.) His business had been carpentry and his firm had built beach huts. The family used one themselves although the beach was in easy walking distance of the house. My grandmother lived with them and she had lost her memory. Often when my aunt, her daughter, appeared, she would nudge me and ask, "Who's she?"

Although I suppose the couple were kind enough to me, I had the feeling that he was trying to smarten or toughen me up, or even improve me. He didn't exactly make me march left, right, left, right, but I always had the feeling that I didn't come up to his standards. He gave me books to

Pat's younger brother, Alistair, with a family friend

Pat with Mary
'The Laundry' (centre)

Alistair, aged 3

Pat (right) and his younger
brother Malcolm and family friend

In Miss Alina's class (Primary 3). Back row, 4th from left.

In Mr MacKenzie's class (early Secondary). Back row, 6th from left.

Pat at 16 Scotland Street in the
early 1950s

Pat's father, Malcolm,
during the Great War

Chapter 3

People and Personalities

I have been thinking about the various people who lived in this little part of Scotland Street and Keith Street and the interesting and varied paths that they and their offspring followed. Next door to each other on Keith Street were the Macleods and the Macleans. Bunty Macleod married Ron, an accountant, and they spent most of their lives in Africa where Ron was Auditor General and Accountant General of different countries of the Central Africa Federation at various times. Latterly he was Dr Banda's right hand man as Accountant General of Malawi. The Malawian bank notes carried Ron's signature at that time.

Bunty herself was head of an insurance company for a period. Their son Christopher was also an accountant and became the head of the international finance company, Lonrho, in Africa. Lonrho was headed by 'Tiny' Rowland who, rightly or wrongly, was described in the House of Commons as 'the unacceptable face of international capitalism!'

Anna Maclean's son Alistair Darling is, of course, a former Chancellor of the Exchequer. It is strange that two little girls, growing up as neighbours on Keith Street, should become the mothers of high ranking financial figures!

Anna's sister, Morag, left Keith Street when she married John Angus Maciver who became Head Master of Stornoway Primary School. Whilst captain of a destroyer during the Second World War, John Angus had the experience of accepting the formal surrender of the captain and crew of a German warship. Morag was herself a teacher and linguist. Their son, Ian, held a senior position in the National Library of Scotland for many years. He was a real gentleman; sadly he died in 2007. Their other son, Kenneth, is a sheriff (not the kind with a star and a Colt.45!).

Also from Keith Street was Compton Macleod, who retired as a headmaster, and (voluntarily) took up the entertainment of tourists on buses, and maybe planes and ships for all I know. His sisters were Hetty and Alice Ann. The latter went once to America to visit her daughter and emerged from the plane like a blue-eyed film star, carrying a huge bouquet of flowers, presented by the plane's crew. She must have entertained them well, as she certainly could.

On Scotland Street lived the Smith family who had previously lived in a tenement type of building on Keith Street which people called 'the Hogg'. It was named after a naval training depot at the Battery which was called *HMS Hogg*. A lot of the RNRs who trained there had stayed at the house in Keith Street, hence the nickname. All the subsequent residents of this house were called 'Hogglers', a rather unattractive-sounding nickname; it is understandable that those called it did not like it.

The Smiths who moved to Scotland Street 'took in' lodgers. A man looking for a room was directed to the house. Katy opened the door, and the man enquired politely, "Miss Hoggler?"

"Smith is the name to you!" she bellowed, with probably a few more choice words. The man fled for his life.

Katy had, very likely, some spots of human tenderness in her nature, but most of us would call her 'formidable'. On another occasion, she wasn't feeling very well so she went across the road to Dr Angus and requested 'a tonic' (her own diagnosis). "Alright," said Dr Angus, "but I'll just sound your chest first; open your blouse a little, Katy."

At that, she bawled, "Who do you think you are? Lady Chatterley's lover?" The partition between the surgery and the waiting area was rather flimsy at the time, so the other patients were highly amused by this episode.

There were other lifelong friends – two sisters - on Keith Street, who lived in a large, cold house built by their father in the late 1800s. He was also involved in the building of the High Church. The sisters lived a Spartan existence: nothing in the house had changed since it was built, even the wallpaper. They lived to an advanced age despite the lack of a Social Work Department in those days to come to their aid in their declining years. They lost four brothers, either in the trenches or as a result of war wounds, in the First World War.

They seemed to do everything in slow motion, accompanied by a tuneless humming. On New Year's Day, only, they lit a fire in their front room and would sit on either side of it, legs crossed at the knee, humming quietly to themselves, like a scene from a play called 'Waiting for Gentlemen Callers.'

To celebrate the New Year I usually took some sherry round to them and would sit shivering, although they didn't seem to feel the cold. There was a piano in the room but the keys were stuck with the damp. The sisters had good voices and were a part of the choir which went to London and won the Lovat and Tullibardine Shield.

On one particular 1st of January, I asked them to bring glasses for the sherry and, while these were being fetched, I slipped a few lumps of coal from the scuttle onto the fire. By the time they came back the fire had started to blaze, frightening them. "Did you do that?" asked one. "And will you put it out if the house catches fire?" She then got the shovel, scooped the burning coal out of the fire, and threw the lot out into the snow!

Although they were sometimes a bit 'nippy', they were kind people. I'm sorry that the community did not do more to help them in their final years.

Bobby Campbell, one of the large family known as the 'Kylers', grew up on Scotland Street. Against advice, he left school at 14, probably to start earning money. He worked in offices, including a solicitors, and was obviously smart, quick to learn and with a good memory. From the solicitors, he was called up to be a 'Bevin' boy in England. He had an office job, meaning that he did not have to go down the mines.

After the War he went to Cape Town, South Africa, where he answered an advert from BP Oils and convinced them that he could do the job they wanted. When asked where he had studied, he replied, "The University of Life!" He was hired, which was very lucky for him as, by this time, he was actually down to his last few shillings.

The job involved travelling in South Africa and as far north as Rhodesia. In Bulawayo he met a contingent of Stornoway folk including Bunty Macleod, Dodi Mackenzie ('Craggan') from Laxdale and Kenny 'Coachy' Maclennan. Both Dodi and Coachy worked in banks. He also met Jacky Mackenzie, a teacher from Coll, Marjory Maciver, ex Barvas Lodge, and the Mayor who was a brother of Willie John the Butcher. On their visits home, these folk told about the entertainment they got with Bobby on his visits to the city with his stories of his adventures on his travels. (Margaret, his widow, said that some of his stories were not to be believed as he embroidered them to entertain his listeners!) They were amazed at the knowledge he had acquired after only three years of secondary education.

Bobby and Margaret met on the ship he was taking home after his first spell in South Africa. Margaret was an officer on the ship. She says he often managed to sit at the Captain's table; in fact, on one occasion, the Captain sought out Bobby's table – he obviously enjoyed his yarns, whether fact or fiction!

Later, he got a job as a cashier with Lloyd's Bank in London, which seems amazing as he had no previous experience in this area. After a spell in London he was transferred to Newcastle, before moving on to a Stornoway bank.

In a change of career, he then went on to run a boarding house in Kingussie with accommodation for 22 guests.

On his second trip to South Africa he worked for a firm called General Leasing which, among other things, leased aeroplanes. His last move was to the Roads Department of Dundee City Council, from which he retired in 2004.

A lack of further education certainly did not hold him back. Of course, he had an excellent partner in his wife, Margaret, who went along with all his moves and travels, creating comfortable homes wherever they went.

An interesting annual event on Keith Street came with the arrival of spring. This was announced by a smoke signal from the garden behind Danny and Annie Macleod's house. On the first sunny day in April, Annie would decide that the time had come, and on went a bonfire of the winter's rubbish, or what she classed as rubbish. It was worthwhile looking out for Danny's arrival from work, and then going over to Mrs Sime's garden next door on the pretext of getting a few stalks of her rhubarb.

Suddenly, a bellow from Danny would be heard. "Why did you burn my boots?" to which there would be a quiet murmur from Annie at the kitchen window. "They were full of holes…"

"They were nothing of the sort. I was keeping them for the peats." There would be silence for a minute or two, then another shout from Danny, "My good jacket! That would have done for years."

"It was twenty years old and done for," would come Annie's reply.

"And what about that tin of paint?" Danny would roar.

"It was nearly empty," Annie would reply.

"It was half full," Danny would retort.

Soon, the sound of a long stick scrabbling among the embers would be heard as Danny tried to rescue 'precious' belongings.

Danny was very kind to his elderly neighbours, giving them tea in bed and setting their fires before heading off to his work. One of his unforgettable neighbours was 'Teens'. She had endless stories of Stornoway in the 19th century and a visitor's head could be sore with laughter after a visit to her.

Once an old Stornoway salt, I think his name was Billy Woggan, decided to retire from the sea to the place of his roots. He was visiting Mrs Whittaker's shop, passing the time after his many years at sea. "Why don't you settle down and get married?" asked Mrs Whittaker, who had what they call 'pawky' humour.

"Who would marry me?" asked Billy.

"What about Teens Maclean?" suggested the mischief...sorry matchmaker. (Teens was probably a grandmother by this time!)

So, one Wednesday afternoon, Billy knocked on Teens's door. Of course, they were old acquaintances, so she greeted him and welcomed him home, but said, "I'm afraid I can't ask you in because I'm engaged." Teens actually had Canon Meaden from the Episcopalian Church in for tea every Wednesday afternoon.

The next time Billy saw Mrs Whittaker he said, "What do you mean, sending me to Teens Maclean when she's engaged?"

Teens was widowed very young but lived to her late 80s or 90s. She had an excellent memory for people and stories, but it failed her on one occasion. Talking generally about her early life, I happened to mention her husband. She thought for a minute, and then repressed a slight giggle. "You know," she said, "I can't remember him!"

I supposed that if he had died in his twenties, after two World Wars and the loss of her son at eighteen in the Iolaire tragedy, there would naturally be a certain blanking out of memories. There were unlikely to be many photographs to preserve memories in these times.

One of her funny stories was about two young men of the 'travelling' clan who, it seems, had been having fisticuffs down town. These tiffs were quite good to watch, but were mostly 'pretend' as fists did not often make contact. This time, the fight developed into the pursuit of one man by the other, along Cromwell Street and Bayhead, up New Street, and into Keith Street where, finally and to escape capture, the pursued man sought sanctuary by diving into Teens's little sitting room. Poor Teens was trapped inside, while the fight continued around her. There were no fatalities, and it was a good story to tell when it was all over.

Another story with Keith Street connections concerned relatives of Maggie Bow's. A girl in the Lochs district had been persuaded by her father to marry a man she didn't particularly want to. On the day of the marriage in Gravir church, the fisherman whom the girl really wanted to be with arrived back from a sea trip. When he heard what was happening, he jumped back into his boat and sailed round to Gravir. He marched into the church where the couple were standing in front of the minister, lifted the girl in his arms and marched out. As they made their escape, one woman hissed, "You should be ashamed of yourself!"

The girl replied, "I don't care. I got the one with the gumboots." Apparently, the one left at the altar was above wearing gumboots. After such a romantic start, fortunately, the couple went on to have a very happy marriage.

On Scotland Street in part of the Seminary building lived two elderly sisters, widows of two brothers. The 'youngish' sister was in her 80s, with the older one – who only spoke Gaelic – in her 90s. The younger one liked to make out that she was very modern, but did not approve of lipstick or 'sticklip' as she called it! She also translated for her sister although her own English was somewhat fractured.

On Sundays they wore what must have been traditional fashions: long black dresses and cloaks and, their pride and joy, high elaborate hats, decorated with beads and tied under their chins. When they went down the street on a windy Sunday with the cloaks spread out like sails they looked a little like 'wherries', setting sail for the fishing grounds, apart from the hats!

The younger sister died first and, lo and behold, perfect English started flowing out of the mouth of the older sister. It seemed that she just never got a chance to use it because her sister was somewhat domineering. At her 100th birthday party the guests were in two rooms. In the other room I could hear the birthday girl being interviewed by a reporter (Kenny Nicolson's wife, Zena). She was asked a question about the secret of her longevity and I heard her responding in English! I said to her later, "To think of all the sore heads I have had over the years, trying to speak to you in Gaelic!"

Round the corner on Keith Street was the Macrae family who, because of their calling (undertakers), had developed the ability to pull people's legs and make jokes while maintaining suitably solemn faces.

Duncan Morison lived opposite them. Once he bought a load of peats and I decided to try to stack them for him whilst he was in school as I knew he would have even less idea than I had about how to do this. In any case, his hands had to be protected for the music!

I had half the stacking done when Archie Macrae came over with a very solemn look on his face. "Hey, you're putting them in the wrong way!" he said. Demonstrating on a peat, he continued, "This is the side you put in to keep the rain out and let the wind dry them. You'll have to take the whole thing down and start again."

"No fear!" said I, before I caught the glimpse of a twinkle in his eye as he walked away.

Al was a bit the same, as is Archie Junior, but the best (or worst!) was Rena. She used to wander round our shop, picking up objects and looking at the prices. "Robbery; daylight robbery!" she would say, with a smile of course. One day, Rena spied a customer, obviously not local, paying for a purchase out a wallet packed with notes. She sidled over to him saying, "Hello, sailor!" At this, the man snapped his wallet shut and scuttled out of the shop, looking over his shoulder with a frightened look on his face. Rena, of course, looked as solemn as ever, but the girls in the shop were highly amused.

Another day, Rena was in the shop when a man stuck his head in the door and shouted to Maggie, a staff member, "See you later. Same place!"

Rena drawled, "It's the queer people you know!"

"That's my husband," said Maggie, much amused.

Talking of Rena reminds me of another performer, Sandra Nicolson, who looked to me like someone you would see in Paris; very slim, often in black slacks and with a beret at a jaunty angle. You could sometimes see her on the pavement with a brush or duster, supposedly busy, but this was just a stance so she could catch some 'victims' to have some fun with by exercising her sharp wit. If you were on the receiving end, you either had to take it and run, or try to give as good in return. Sparks used to fly between her and her father, Tommy, but he didn't mind because he was a blacksmith!

When he became quite old he used to go down town with a trolley with a list and money inside to get some things for Sandra. He probably wanted to feel useful for as long as possible. A little boy in the neighbourhood had become fascinated by funerals. He was probably about four, and could often be seen on the pavement, open-mouthed, gazing at the spectacle. One day, Tommy was crawling up Scotland Street when he noticed the little boy, standing and staring at him. He grunted a greeting at the lad, whose innocent response was, "When's your funeral going to be?"

Further down the street lived Mrs Mackinnon. Although she was very deaf, she 'took in lodgers'- collar and tie gents only, if you please! She also kept a few hens. One day, she was having an afternoon tea party. As she left the room to make the refreshments the conversation was about hens. When she returned, the talk had turned to lodgers but she hadn't realised this.

"How many have you got just now, Mrs Mackinnon?" asked one lady, interested in her neighbour's lodgers.

"Six," came the reply, "and none of them are laying!"

A lady who lived at the bottom of Keith Street in a flat near the corner of South Beach and James Street had a pet parrot. On many weekends, group of revellers leaving the Imperial Hotel, would swing round the corner in a horse-drawn cart, usually singing Gaelic songs. No doubt it was quite a din, and if the woman's window was open she was in the habit of shouting, "Oh, shut up, you drunken Rubhachs…!" The parrot, woken by the noise, would move back and forth on his perch, repeating his owner's words.

When the woman died, a wake was held in her house. The parrot was pushed into a corner. The psalm singing had just started when the bird interrupted proceedings, squawking, "Shut up, you drunken Rubhachs!"

Another example of Stornoway humour involved two lady residents having a gossip in the street in the middle of their morning chores. They spied a lady from suburbia swinging down Scotland Street, all dressed up and carrying an article of dress called a muff. This was usually made of fur and was shaped like a tube with open ends, so that the hands could be inserted for warmth. One of the on- looking ladies turned to the other and said with more than a touch of scorn, "Huh, look at her with a muff on a Monday!"

I must not forget to mention a personality who lived in Scotland Street for many years, a lady known as Mrs Peter. She was the second wife and widow of Peter Macleod, also known as Peter 'Smart'. The 'Smart' family owned businesses and property in Stornoway, the last being J. & E. Macleod's on the corner of Kenneth Street and Church Street. Mrs Macleod could well have had the nickname 'Smart' herself because she was what was called 'capable'. She walked in a business-like way, long skirt swishing and one arm swinging. In fact, she was slightly intimidating. Neighbours were inclined to make a quick tidy of their house if they heard her approaching. But she was very kind to people when they had 'trouble', to the extent of bringing in hot meals to those who were looking after patients. If illness proved too serious and you had to depart, she was an expert in 'laying you out'.

She kept a cow, and the young girls whom she employed as maids had to the march the animal, every day, to its grazing place, and then escort it home every night to be milked. These girls certainly got good training in a number of domestic skills.

Mrs Peter ruled the roost in our area. If she shouted at us boys, "Get down off that wall!" by golly, we got down!

As age advanced, she went to live with her daughter in Glasgow. As her house was let or sold, she left various articles with friends for safe-keeping, where they stayed for years. I made a big blunder concerning one of these items. At one time, prominent male citizens in Stornoway wore very formal clothes on special occasions such as funerals. Peter Smart's morning suit and top hat, in a cardboard box, had been left in our house. It had been there for some years when I decided that I would dress up in the suit and hat and make an entrance downstairs, causing a surprise and maybe raising a laugh. So, I crept down the stairs which were almost opposite the front door and, just before I reached the bottom, the door opened and who walked in but Mrs Peter, home on holiday to visit her sister.

She looked me up and down with the most withering expression I ever saw before she stepped into the living room. I skulked back upstairs and stayed there until she left. To give her her due she did not mention the incident and nothing was ever said to me about it, but what a coincidence!

Mrs Peter's daughter, Bella, was a nice looking lady and had a strong personality like her mother. She married a ship's captain who courted her in the shop they owned after her father died. They lived in Glasgow after they married. Some time after that I met him coming out of an establishment in the town, looking happy and wiping his mouth. He told me that, being at sea most of his working life, he never spent more than two weeks at a time with Bella and never got involved in the usual landlubbers' activities like sport. One time he was at home he was passing the time doing odd jobs about the house. He decided to make a new path to the back door and spent a whole morning smoothing the cement. Suddenly, Bella appeared loaded up to her chin with washing for the line. Before he could warn her she had stepped onto his newly made path. He shouted some unsuitable words that annoyed Bella so much that she told him to go and get another job.

"So, here I am," he said, "first officer on a fishery cruiser with fewer responsibilities than a captain and more pay! I'm having a great time!"

Another drama that I got involved in on Scotland Street could easily have had fatal consequences if it had not been for a series of coincidences. The situation happened in a large house where three elderly sisters lived. They were all disabled: one could not walk at all but could get about the house by crawling. She always carried a duster in her pocket and indicated to any visitors where her sisters were by pointing it. Another one could only walk with support while the third sister could walk very slowly but only within the house. I don't remember what sort of help they had, but my contribution for a number of years was to take breakfast rolls to them every morning. They were very independent and determined to carry on as best they could. They seemed to be nervous about doctors, probably afraid they would be taken into a care home. There was not much of a selection of these then!

The house had been converted into four flats. The sisters used the two upstairs ones and rented out the two below. A new staircase had been made for access to the upstairs flats via a fairly steep, narrow stair with no window to the outside, and a sliding door at the bottom leading to a small lobby.

By this stage, a mishap had befallen the 'middle' sister who had fallen one morning and, according to my 'vast' medical knowledge, had probably dislocated her shoulder, but no doctors were to be sent for. The result was that, in addition to the rolls duties, I had to help her get into a sitting position in the mornings. From there she could manage herself, possibly with help from the slightly mobile sister after I left. Now come the coincidences.

One evening I had just arrived home when one of the Henderson boys from Bayhead came to the door. He said he had been sent by a lady who had asked for me as there had been an accident up the road. Looking up the street, I saw Mrs Emily Macdonald standing on the pavement outside the sisters' house. Mrs Macdonald was a Londoner married to a doctor who was distantly related to the three ladies in the house. She was very particular about the correct time to 'pay calls'. On the evening in question she realised that she had neglected to call on the sisters to say goodbye as she and her husband were going on holiday the following day. It was almost too late to catch Nana before she closed the sliding door for the night, but she decided to try.

She found she could not open the door and, when she tried, there were groans from behind the door. So she sent for me. At first, I couldn't think what to do. Neither of us thought of trying to phone the police, and it was just as well, as it would have been too late. By a stroke of luck, I remembered that there was an unused lean-to added to the upstairs kitchen at the back of the house, with rickety wooden stairs attached to it. It was never used and always kept locked. A window halfway up the stairs looked beyond my reach. I thought that it was probably stuck shut with paint or age, as with a lot of windows in old properties like my own.

With a bit of a jump I managed to get my fingers onto to the ledge and started to claw and scratch my way up the roughcast using my knees, toes and maybe my nose (it wasn't much of a nose to begin with and was not the better for the experience!). At last I got my forearms onto the ledge and managed to try the window. It was the sash and case type, and – you won't believe this- it flew open like magic! Nana had got the joiner round that very day to have the window unstuck – an amazing coincidence.

I then managed to get in the window to an unused bedroom which fortunately was unlocked, and from there through the house to the stairs. On the way, I passed the sitting room and heard my name being called. "Pat! Lift me! Lift me!"

Inside the room I saw Jessie, who could not walk at all, lying flat on the floor, face downwards. She obviously knew there was something wrong and had tried to get up but had fallen flat. "I have to help Nana first," I said.

"No, me first," she insisted. She obviously did not want to be found in that situation. She had had a number of falls and it always took two to lift her. I'm amazed to think I found the strength to heave her up and almost throw her into a chair before dashing to the stairs.

Mary, the third sister, was sitting at the top, unable, of course, to do anything. Poor Nana had been on her way to lock up, tripped and fell headlong down this steep, narrow stair, so that she was lying full length down the stairs, with her head trapped between the sliding door and the lowest step. Her face was changing colour and she was breathing with difficulty. Her whole weight was on her head and neck and she was quite a large lady. I knew that you were not supposed to lift anyone who had had a bad fall, but, as it looked as though she was choking, I had to free her head. I pulled back on her shoulders and, taking the pressure off it, managed to slide the door open. She began to breathe easier and seemed to become conscious. Then the problem was to move her very carefully down the stairs into the small lobby. By opening the front door I finally managed to get her into a sitting position. She was eventually able to speak a little and said she had no pain.

I told Mrs Macdonald, who was standing by, to support her while I dashed upstairs to get a drink (for her, not me). I made a very quick cup of tea which really made a difference to her recovery. This is the real water of life (not the other stuff!).

Then there was the problem of getting her back upstairs. After giving her some time to recover, I got her sitting up on the lowest step. It took a long time, but I helped her to go upstairs backwards on her bottom. At the top, I left her in the charge of one or two ladies who had gathered, and went home to recover myself, although, of course, no doctor was to be called.

There was a sequel to this story. I had noticed little boxes in a few windows around the town and learnt that they contained a red light which could be used to summon help in an emergency. I thought this was a good idea and was told that I should see Mrs Dart of the Red Cross to arrange for one for the ladies after Nana's close call. Although I thought the ladies, who were very private, would have to be prepared for this, Mrs Dart, who stood no nonsense, insisted on going round right away to fit the gadget. When we arrived, the ladies had friends in and were obviously relating the near disaster of the previous evening. Our arrival created a small sensation. Mrs Dart showed Jessie, who was chair-bound, all she had to do to work it; by pressing a button and without getting out of her chair, help could be summoned- Jessie was quite intrigued!

The next day, she was having fun showing visitors the new gadget. Unfortunately, she forgot to switch it off. That evening, Magga, a friend who lived close by and had seen the demonstration, was on her way to bed and looked out the window to her friends' house as she always did to check that all was well there. What did she see but the Red Cross light flashing in their window! Down she went as fast as she could to the house next door where there was a young policeman in digs. "Come quickly," she said. "There's something wrong in the Macarthurs'!"

On went his jacket and he made a dash across the street, followed by Magga, as fast as she could go, which wasn't very fast because her legs were starting to go. The sliding door was locked. Obviously Nana had been down doing her nightly security check, despite her recent near-disaster.

I'm not sure how he did it, because I wasn't there, but he got in and bounded up the narrow stairs, and was met by Nana at the top, shouting, "Who are you? What are you doing in my house?"

"I'm a policeman and this old lady told me there was a light flashing in your window," he replied, enraging Magga who certainly didn't consider herself to be old!

"And how did you get into my house?" asked Nana.

"I broke a window and opened the latch on the door," said he.

"You broke a window," yelled Nana. "And will you pay for it?"

The poor young man retorted, "I suppose someone will. Maybe the old lady here?"

This was too much for Magga who interrupted, "Excuse me. I am NOT an old lady."

I suppose eventually they all went back to their own beds. And, I suppose, I was blamed. What comes from trying to do the right thing!

I made another blunder a few years later. I think the two older sisters had passed away as Nana was on her own. I was passing the house one evening and saw the bedroom light on. As Nana usually sat in the sitting room at that time, I decided to pop in to see how she was. The sliding door wasn't locked which was a bad sign. When I went in, she was in bed and very sad.

"I'm going. I'm finished," she said. "Apart from the nurse you are the only person I have seen today." She continued, "And that woman down the stairs who puts her hat on to come up to draw the curtains. And look how she does that!"

The neighbour obviously just gave one quick pull to each side with no arranging of the drapes. Nana was such a particular person that even although she was 'going' or 'finished', she wanted the curtains arranged properly. She ordered me to do it as best she could. She then asked me to give her a spoonful of medicine. I had just got new bi-focal glasses which change the way you see things as you move your eyes. So, instead of ending up in her mouth, the medicine spilled down her nice bed jacket. She, being particular, was very upset. I went for a cloth and left her to it. Looking back, I'm very sorry it happened.

I really admired these three ladies for their courage in hanging on to their independence from hospitals and care homes for so long.

There are many stories about another local resident who became very well known in his long life, especially in the world of Scottish and Hebridean music. Duncan 'Major' Morison first played on a toy piano, then a pedal organ, then a keyboard and eventually a piano. He got a little professional help and soon learnt to sight read. His first public performance was in school.

During a Maths lesson with John Macrae (or Johnny Crae who went on to be the Rector), Duncan wasn't paying attention because he could only hear the music coming from the music room. Suddenly Johnny Crae pounced:

"What is that, Morison?" he demanded, referring to something on the board.

"Ode to Joy, sir," replied Duncan.

"Stay behind after the class," said Johnny Crae who was known as a strict disciplinarian. Duncan sat in fear and trembling. After the class was dismissed, he said to Duncan, "Would you play at the assemblies on Monday morning?"

What a relief! This was to be his first experience of playing in public. The next few years were taken up with small jobs; playing at dances in the Wydo Dance Band, and accompanying silent films in Will Mack's cinema next to his house for 7/6d a week. He took over after the dismissal of his predecessor following the 'Birkenhead' episode I mentioned earlier. Duncan never picked the wrong tune: in cowboy films, the Indians rode bareback with a jerky, bouncy motion. The cowboys used a saddle so the movement was slower. Duncan had appropriate tunes for each.

He then got some financial help from his brother, Louis, in Malaya, and went for a short time to the Academy of Music and Drama. It was quite difficult for him to start this course at his age as he was in twenties and had developed a recognisable style. At home and in the city he was much in demand as an accompanist, and this may have affected his studies.

He heard that the Marchioness of Londonderry had given the use of the ballroom in her London mansion to the London Gaelic Choir to have a concert to raise funds for the Lewis Hospital. He was desperate to be included on the programme and wrote to the Secretary of the Choir, whom he knew as she had begun life a few yards from his own home. He had a bit of a disappointment when she refused him. She had 'risen in the world' since going to London, working as an accountant, marrying a sea captain and, then, working at raising money for charities. Later she became a Dame. Perhaps she had not realised what Duncan had already achieved as a pianist.

However, nothing daunted, Duncan wrote to Dame Flora Macleod of Macleod whom he had become acquainted with at events in Glasgow and at Highland concerts. She wrote to 'Lady L' who decided that, "This young man must have a chance," and persuaded the Secretary of the Choir to put him on the programme.

This was the start of Duncan's new life! He had practised some pieces for his performance, but listening to some of the earlier performances, he realised that they were pretty good and changed his plan. He played some traditional pieces with his own arrangements, and one or two originals of his own. He probably included some of the modernised Kennedy Fraser songs, which wouldn't have pleased the traditionalists but would have been popular with most of the audience. One favourite was 'Mairi's Wedding March' which he described as the Lewis Bridal Procession March. This sounded very grand, but those 'in the know' in the audience would have recognised that in the days before cars everyone had to walk to the church – hardly a procession!

I can easily imagine him taking the stage in his Highland finery (kilt, jacket with silver buttons and lace at the cuffs) and his head slightly tilted up. He made quite an impression, and Lady L obviously liked his style!

Sandra Nicolson, another entertaining personality whom I mentioned earlier, lived opposite Major at the junction of Scotland Street and Keith Street. For a time after her father died, Sandra had people staying for Bed and Breakfast. Two such were young men who were travelling in the islands on behalf of some religious organisation. After some time in Sandra's house, they decided to get a tent and move out, probably to save the expense.

On their first night out there was a big storm and their tent blew away. They came back to Sandra's soaking wet to see if she would take them back. As they stepped into the hall with their wet shoes, Sandra bawled, "Get off that rug! That's a prayer mat!" They leapt in the air and off the mat. Then they caught a glimpse of Sandra's secret smile.

At one time, Sandra had a cat called Marmalade on account of her colour. She was well known in the locality for producing illegitimate kittens for which Sandra blamed my cat. She threatened to dump the next batch on my doorstep. Whoever the rascally father was, it couldn't have been mine as that was a 'she' as well. Fortunately she always found good homes for them.

She had a young girl in digs with her at this time. Late one evening she was asked to go and call Marmalade in for the night. I suppose the young lady did not like to stand shouting "Marmalade!" so she called "Puss! Puss!" instead. There was no response so she closed the door. A man in the next street had the nickname 'Pushy' and he used to pass Sandra's on his way home from his evening's entertainment in town. There was a little knock on the door, and here he was. "Was someone calling me?" he asked, hopefully. It would have made a nice change for him to be invited in to Sandra's, but I'm afraid he had to go home disappointed!

When Marmalade eventually died, a quiet, reserved lady neighbour met her as she passed her door. "Good morning, Sandra. I'm sorry about poor Marmalade. What happened to her?"

"What will never happen to you or me, Murdina. She died having kittens."

Poor Murdina ran off with her hands over her ears!

After she had been on her own for some time, Sandra decided to sell the house. She got a job on the mainland near to her sister, Bessie, who taught in a small rural school where her husband was Headmaster. Sandra became housekeeper and companion to a lady with serious health problems. Unfortunately, this lady came to a tragic end in the Rubislaw quarry. She had been very happy with Sandra but her illness had been too much for her.

Shortly after this, I visited Sandra at Bessie's house. Whilst I was there, a letter came for her from a noble lord who owned a large estate in the area, inviting her to his stately home for afternoon tea. Sandra waved the letter around, shouting, "Who is this? How does he know me? Why does he want to see me?"

Bessie, who had a slightly similar personality, gave her sisterly advice. "Well, Sandra, if he wants you as a concubine on a cruise on his yacht, you just go!" Sandra did go, but as a companion and help. The noble lord was in his eighties and had heard of Sandra from a tenant farmer whose sister had been the lady who had died tragically in the quarry. Sandra had obviously been described as someone who would be good company.

He sometimes entertained other aristocrats and VIPs. Sandra arranged the dinners and took her place at the table with the guests. They would have been well entertained. She felt completely at ease in any company and would not have been concerned about class differences. I can easily imagine her asking, "And what do you do for a living?" Probably most of them did not have to work!

I don't know how long she stayed there, but she would certainly have livened up that castle. It was fairly isolated, so eventually she moved back to the city. She phoned now and again after she left the lord in his castle. I once tried to persuade her to come to Stornoway for a holiday.

"Stornoway?" she bawled. "I'll be lucky to make it to the crematorium!"

Rena Macrae was another colourful and entertaining personality in our neighbourhood. Her funny stories were further improved by her dramatic face and expressive voice. One story was about a telephone call she received early one morning before she left for work. The caller said, "I'm sorry to bother you so early but I'm in a bit of a fix. I came to town from South Lochs yesterday to buy a ram at the auction and it is being delivered today."

"You have the wrong number, I'm afraid," said Rena. "I'm only a typist in a solicitor's office. I know nothing about rams. In fact, I'm terrified of them and wouldn't go near one for a hundred pounds."

"I phoned because I knew your father had a phone for his business (the undertaker's). My problem is," continued the caller, "that I have an appointment with the dentist this morning to get all my teeth extracted. I can't chew anything anymore with them. Then I have to go home on the bus and they won't let me take the ram with me. So I have tied it to a drain pipe round the back of 16 Scotland Street."

"What!" shrieked Rena. "I won't even walk past the house if it's there! Why have you left it there? What if it escapes?"

"A lady from my village works in a weaving shed there. She won't have arrived yet but I will have to go for my appointment. I'm looking for someone to go and tell her to find someone to walk the ram down to the quay to the *True Love*. If it escapes there will be an awful lot of lambs born at New Year when nobody wants them. I would like to be sure that he is well tethered on the boat and his legs are tied. He is a big, strong animal and if he jumps around he could capsize a small fishing boat."

"Why all this fuss about a ram?" asked Rena. "Are there not plenty in your part of the world?"

"The one we had is done for, like my teeth," was the answer. "And if this one is lost over the side, I'll be done for. That ram cost a fortune and I'm the clerk of the Grazing Committee."

"Oh, well," said Rena. "I'm off to work and I'll have to round by Francis Street in case I meet that ram. I'll leave a message for my father."

I don't know what Peggy, the weaver, thought when she saw the ram, but it must have reached Cromore and lived happily ever after!

Years later, a friend of mine had been advised to take up an energetic activity for health reasons. Scottish Country Dancing was suggested and he asked me to accompany him. As I am known to be hopeless at such things, I suspected that everyone else he had asked had refused. Anyway, he talked me into it and off we went to Matheson Hall, where I had suffered that injustice on my very first day in school, and had avoided ever since.

61

Approaching the door and peeping in, we saw a motley gang of people, some of whom we knew, of different ages and sizes, tripping round the room as if playing 'Ring-a-ring-of-roses', trying to learn the steps for reels and strathspeys. Frieda Parker, the gym teacher, was in the middle, keeping an eye on the novices.

Murdo and I decided to escape but Frieda had spied us and hauled us in. I must have got the idea quite quickly but my friend was soon tying his feet in knots. This was his one and only attempt, but I kept going and learnt a few dances. My worst blunder came in the Dashing White Sergeant. As some readers will know, groups of three dancers go round the hall in different directions; when two groups meet, one lot raise their arms and the others go under. One time, I wasn't thinking and, instead of bending and going under, I slapped a lady in the face. She forgave me a few years later!

The sequel to all this is that, some time later, 'word' was sent round the town that a keen Scottish Country dancer had arrived in Stornoway and was eager to collect a group to come to his house regularly to dance. I was roped in, of course. They had a huge room, possibly two made into one, with only one article of furniture: a small bureau topped with a timetable of the dances we were going to do, and diagrams of the steps of the different dances. This could have been a knitting pattern for all the sense it made to me. As usual, I just went to the end of the set and watched the experts.

On that first night, as we had entered the house, who should I have seen in the garden next door but Rena. She stopped what she was doing to stare at the little procession. As I passed, she called me and whispered, "What's all this? Where are you going?"

"We're going to dance," says I. Seeing her quizzical look at the variety of performers, I explained how the invitation had come about.

"The next time I'm coming in to watch," she threatened.

Sure enough, the next night we gathered at the house, my old friend from Keith Street was sitting in a small alcove from where she could observe the dances. "Don't worry," she said. "I'll go home at the interval." There was always a tea-break.

It was very hard for me to concentrate on the dancing because I could see Rena's face, especially when it all went wrong! Occasionally one person would make a mistake and the whole lot would jumble. Everyone, except our host who took it all very seriously, would find this quite funny. There was one particular dancer who really shouldn't have been there at all. He was going round gasping for breath, mouth open, trying his best to keep up with the steps and the music. When you reach a certain age and size, and lose your waist, and are slightly knock-kneed, you should not try Scottish Country Dancing. This stout dancer wore a kilt that he must have had when he was young and slim; now it barely reached his knees. "That kilt is going to fall down!" predicted Rena. I assured her that it was probably hooked on to safety pins or braces. In the days of open fires, people used to say, in reference to useless objects which were past their best, "I just put it to the back of the fire." That's what should have happened to that kilt!

Anyway, it was all good fun and Rena enjoyed being the audience. Of course she had to hide her laughter which she saved for later when she was telling others the story.

Peggy 'Fido' at the loom at the back of 16 Scotland Street

Calum MacDonald, the visitor from Canada who had lived
next door as a boy

Chapter 4

The War

There were a lot of unusual meetings and coincidences during the war. I suppose there were bound to be given the concentration of service personnel in ships and camps around the world, but it was always a great surprise when two people who knew each other well in another environment came face to face by chance thousands of miles away. For instance, one day I was rushing – or trying to rush- along a crowded street in Cairo. I was late for an appointment at the Jewish Club which was a popular place to eat. I had hitchhiked across the desert, but did not think that my brother would wait too long for me. Suddenly, I bumped into a soldier. Who was it but my friend from school and the Scouts, Dougie Wallace!

I told him where I was going and who I was going to meet and he came along. My brother was asleep in the foyer, with his mouth open. "You wake him," I said to Dougie. It was funny to see the expression on the face of the 'sleeping beauty' when he woke up!

On another occasion when I was an eighteen year old rookie, a number of us were detailed for guard duty on the perimeter of an unoccupied RAF camp. Our instructions were to challenge any suspicious-looking person with, "Halt! Who goes there?" If they did not respond with the password or stop, you were supposed to shoot them! I did think this was not a job for me, who had never even managed to shoot a rabbit, but the fact that they had forgotten to supply us with bullets suggested that we were not trusted! I don't remember how long these shifts lasted, but I had great difficulty in staying awake. Someone told me that if you fell asleep on guard duty you got shot. It was very tedious, so I was pleased when, at the end of my beat, I happened to meet the chap who was patrolling the next beat, especially when he said he was from Skye. It almost seemed like meeting someone from home. However, he was not interested and we did not spend long talking – maybe it was because I was from Lewis!

Sometime later, I was stationed at Dyce and was invited for tea by friends in Aberdeen. During my bus journey, there was an air-raid and the passengers were sent to shelters. I, rather idiotically, decided to keep on walking, otherwise I would be late for my tea. Despite the fact that I could hear metal objects hitting the railings (whether spent cartridge cases, bullets ricocheting, or a German air-gunner taking a pot shot at me!), I reached my destination, the Mennies. They told me there was an airman billeted next door with their neighbours, the Millers, and suggested I go in to see him…I did, and who was there but that Sgiathanach whom I had met 450 miles away on the RAF Base!

The next part of the story is even more amazing: one hot summer afternoon, in a small town square more than 4000 miles away in the Transvaal, a friend and I, off duty, were wandering around in the heat looking for a café for a drink. We were parched, nothing seemed to be open, and no-one was out but us. My friend spotted a sign which said 'TocH' with an arrow pointing through the bushes. I remember the absolute stillness; not even a leaf moved and the birds were silent. I picked an orange from an orange tree, I recall.

TocH was a charitable institution and here provided a hut with a kettle, tea, dried milk and a packet of biscuits. A sign said 'Help yourself. Contributions welcome.' The two of us were sitting having our tea when – you won't believe this- the Sgiathanach wandered in. He nodded to me and said, "Is this all there is to eat?" as he looked at the biscuits. I wouldn't be surprised if I was to meet him on Cromwell Street yet!

On another occasion, I was walking on a very crowded pavement, again in Cairo, when I heard my name being shouted through the noise of the traffic, horns and revving engines. I spied someone waving at me on the other side of the street and recognised Doda MacKenzie (Craggan) from Laxdale. Unfortunately, it was impossible to cross over.

Once I was in a queue in Durban, waiting to be inoculated before going to the Middle East. I felt a tug on my jacket from behind and turned to see John Lachy Macleod from the Manse on Lewis Street. I was very pleased to see him, however briefly.

Thinking about these strange meetings reminds me of how naïve and ignorant of the ways of the world I was at eighteen and in my early twenties. In the Transvaal, I used to go and visit a Macaulay family, originally from Lewis. I bought a small suitcase for these weekend visits. It was made of a kind of wickerwork and was light but strong; I really liked it. Soon after I bought it (I don't think I had even used it), a fellow in a neighbouring room said, "Hey, Mac, I'm going away for a weekend. Could I borrow your suitcase?" I certainly did not want to lend it to him, but I had not yet learned to say no, or to come up with an excuse, so off he went. He never came back. He was posted somewhere else. I suppose with everything else that was going on in the world during the war, it did not really matter, but I felt rather annoyed with myself.

One day, maybe a year later, I was walking on a busy street in Johannesburg, 200 miles away. I remember it was Wanderer Street, near the national stadium. Suddenly, through a break in the crowds, a solitary figure approached. I spied my suitcase, and then, carrying it, the thief himself! You should have seen his face when he recognised me!

"Honestly, I was going to send it back to you," he stammered.

"No, you weren't," said I. "I'll take it now." So I made him empty out his laundry, his toothpaste, his hairbrush and some other rubbish on the pavement, and off I went with my suitcase.... No, that's a lie. That's what I should have done and I regret not doing it. But I do wonder how he felt at being caught red-handed?

I remember another experience from early in the war when I was only about nineteen and had a lot to learn. It happened at a landing ground which was being converted from a civil airport to an RAF base early in the war. One runway was being used and part of the perimeter.

One evening, I was pottering around when an officer called me and said he had a job for me. We walked off along the runway, passing three marks where bombs had fallen. This was unusual as the Luftwaffe considered it a waste of bombs given that the damage could be repaired relatively easily. (A friend of mine had been working on this runway when the first bomb fell. Instinctively, he turned and ran in the opposite direction, not realising that he was running towards the second bomb which fell a few seconds later. He was very shocked but survived.) Anyway, I walked on with this officer, past the marks of the filled-in bomb craters, and he told me that a flight of foreign aircraft would be landing on the runway shortly. The runway lights had not yet been installed and it was getting dark. As the planes had been diverted, they were also likely to be running short of fuel. My job was to switch on the floodlight as soon as I heard the engines of the planes. The only problem was that I didn't know how to operate the floodlight. The officer explained that it was simply an ordinary petrol engine which lit up two bulbs with their reflectors. I panicked as I had never started a petrol engine in my life. The officer said he would show me so we climbed up onto the trailer and he turned on the ignition switch and turned the starting handle.

"You must remember to keep your thumb beside your fingers because if it misfires it can break your wrist," he warned.

"Oh great," I thought.

Then he turned on another switch and two very bright lights came on. He showed me how to focus these along the runway.

"Now you do it," said he. To my surprise, I managed the whole process.

"Now switch everything off. We don't want to attract any unfriendly visitors with this bright light."

I thought to myself, "You are asking me to stand beside this lamp until all the Poles (or was it Czechs? I'm not sure now) land. I'll be a perfect target for some scouting Luftwaffe pilot!"

"As soon as you hear the engines," he explained, "switch on the floodlight and signal a green light to the first aircraft that appears."

Quite apart from being a sitting duck, there was another problem. "How do I signal?" I asked.

"With the Aldus lamp, of course," he replied. "Don't tell me you've never used one?" On hearing my reply, he went on to explain that a green beam meant 'go' or 'come' and red one meant 'no'. "When the first one lands, make sure he is clear of the runway before the next one starts his descent. If he is too close, give him a red signal and make him do another circuit. They are probably short of fuel and keen to land, but if they land too close together there could be a fine pile-up on the runway."

So off my instructor went. I felt like calling him back. If he was so clever, why couldn't he do it himself? Then I heard the engines. At first I couldn't see the markings on the planes, but when I did I was relieved to see there were no swastikas!

I shone a green beam on the first plane and saw the wheels and then the flaps coming down. He came in over my head and made a neat landing. By now, the others were circling around; when I saw the first was clear of the runway, I turned to give a green beam to the next nearest. Suddenly, there was a loud roar and a swoosh, and the second was passing so close over my head that it nearly scraped the Brylcreem off my hair! He hadn't waited for a green signal and had used his own judgement. Maybe no-one had told him about the Aldus lamp!

However, the third was showing signs of following the others, a bit near, I thought, so I gave him a red signal and off he went to do another circuit. I carried on, giving reds and greens until they were all down. I was glad to switch everything off and slip away to my own bunk in case any of them were after my blood for making them do extra circuits.

Thinking it over, I'm still amazed that a total stranger asked me to do such a responsible job without knowing that I could do it. It was, actually, basic air traffic control, using a rookie and an Aldus lamp!

There was, however, a sad sequel to these events which shows how vulnerable we were. A friend from Aberdeen, Bill Pirie, and I were once given a job to do which had some similarities to the floodlight one. Round the coasts of the UK were things called aerial lighthouses, not nearly as high as the usual lighthouses; maybe 20 feet tall. Their purpose was to flash letters of the alphabet as a guide to air navigators during the hours of darkness. Our job was in one of these. I can't remember how these things were powered. Bill was more mechanically minded than I was and we had no difficulty keeping it going.

At first we had no shelter and I certainly didn't feel very safe from marauding 'visitors' from the continent which were becoming more frequent. In the summer, with the longer nights, we were told that once the dawn came we could switch the light off and go to sleep on a nearby farmhouse kitchen floor. This arrangement had been made with the farmer. His children had to step over us in the morning when they were going to get their porridge.

The sad part of the story came on a night when Bill and I were off duty and only one man was covering our duties. He would have recognised the sound of an enemy aircraft coming towards him. He started towards the farmhouse but, sad to say, they got him before he reached safety. Bill and I were never detailed for that duty again, and then we went to different parts of the world.

At one point, I was stationed at Dyce in Aberdeenshire with the other half of the squadron in Stornoway. The squadron was flying Ansons. The younger generation won't remember these planes; they were quite old even then, with two radial engines and an undercarriage that hand to be wound up by turning a handle – no press button then!

A young pilot I knew said to me one day, "We are flying up to Stornoway with some equipment. Would you like to come with us for a quick visit home?"

"Sure," I said, and off we went. I had been before so I knew the usual route. After we took off I knew the person at the controls expected passengers to wind up the wheels, which I did. The weather was a bit cloudy, and I didn't like the look of it. The route planned was to join Loch Maree in the region of Achnasheen and fly along the loch to the Minch. The northern shore of the loch points almost directly to Stornoway.

The hills on each side of the loch were hidden in the clouds at their summits, so we were flying below the cloud cover in a kind of V-shaped tunnel. At one point, the pilot mistook where he was, turning into the wrong glen and having to make a very tight turn. I hoped he would turn back then but, no, he was determined to reach Loch Maree. At last, when the visibility got even worse and the shore of the loch began to disappear, the pilot made the decision to make a tight-angled turn in that confined space. Ansons are not very manoeuvrable and to make a turn you have to bank right over. During this manoeuvre, the plane turned towards the mountain which was suddenly right in front of my eyes. For a few seconds I was looking right at the heather and wild flowers. It was only for a few seconds and there was no time to feel fear or anything else.

Just as suddenly, the aircraft straightened out. The co-pilot said, "I suppose you know we nearly bought it up there. It couldn't have been any nearer a miss."

I was just glad I had made a good job of taking the wheels up!

One of the instruments on the Anson was the airspeed indicator. The pilot needs to know the airspeed for take-off and landing. This is worked by an instrument that sits in a tube on the outside of the fuselage. This metal tube is six to eight inches long and is attached to the underside of the aircraft, facing forwards. When the aircraft is on the ground it is usually covered by a kind of sleeve.

One day, as a result of someone's mistake, one of the planes took off with the sleeve still on. A friend of mine, Paddy Murray, volunteered to hang down from the trapdoor, head first, while two colleagues hung onto his legs. He managed to take the cover off the instrument before the others hauled him back inside. He said it was easy, but I don't think many would have done it!

After I had completed a course as a Link Trainer Instructor, I joined the Reina del Pacifico, a cruise ship which had been converted into a troopship. It was the ship on which former Prime Minister Ramsay Macdonald died, incidentally. As we left a port in the north west of England, a band played on the quay. Did they really have to play 'Will you no come back again'? Or maybe it was 'We're no awa tae bide awa'?

We didn't know where we were going but we guessed that it was somewhere to form a new air school as we were mostly instructors. It was obvious that we were heading south because we had been issued with pith helmets and tropical uniforms. Two navigators in our cabin were able to plot our course so we knew at one point we were near to Iceland and then down to South America, before across to West Africa to refuel. This took us several weeks, going at the pace of the slowest ship in the convoy. All this round-about route was to avoid submarines and Focke Wolfe long distance bombers. It was comforting to see all the escorting destroyers. We were in thick fog for some time which probably helped to keep us safe. Later, I met two fellows in the Lebanon, who had been in a convoy which left soon after ours. They were attacked and had losses.

One of the four in my cabin, Tom, was rather difficult to share with, to say the least. One day he was looking out of the porthole into the fog, when he started yelling, "Periscope! Periscope!" and began scrambling for his life jacket. He bawled, "The bridge! The bridge!" and ran off. I suppose the other three of us should have rushed to our stations, but we couldn't see any sign of a torpedo sneaking towards us, so we just stayed where we were.

Then the other fellow came back, looking embarrassed. It wasn't a periscope. Because of the fog, each boat in the convoy had to trail something behind, causing a spout in the water which was a warning to other ships not to get too close.

However, there was another side to our cabin-mate. Tom was a champion chess player and taught the rest of us to play. It helped to keep our minds off the possibility of being blown up by a torpedo or hit by long-range bombers. Usually, he beat us, but one day he and I were playing a game. I don't know whether he had a temporary loss of concentration,

but suddenly he was up and off. He seemed to catch a few up-currents and in minutes had passed the air-field and was out of sight.

A long time passed. We were just beginning to think we should report him missing when he turned up in a lorry with the glider safely dismantled in the back. He had made a very good landing near an isolated farmhouse, miles from anywhere. He told us that the farm was occupied by three very old people, a couple and the sister of one of them. They had a big orchard but, as they were unable to complete the harvest, the ground was covered with uncollected apples. These were being eaten by pigs. (Pigs are very fond of apples. I often wonder if that is why carnivores who eat pigs usually put apple sauce on the poor creatures.) In the middle of this description, he suddenly said to me, "The old folks on the farm asked about you! They knew your name and where you came from."

I was intrigued. Who the hair-oil (as we used to say in Stornoway) were they? I had no idea but remembered who might be able to help. There was a couple, Mr and Mrs Jouber, in a nearby village with a grocery shop. I asked them if they knew the old folk on the farm and they told me that they occasionally delivered groceries to them. They promised to take me with them the next time they went.

So, I saw the orchard and the pigs, and met the old folk. They had no connection with Stornoway themselves, but were very friendly with a couple from Johannesburg, the Macdonalds, who came from the town. Mr Macdonald was a brother of the well-known Stornoway personality, Murdo Gow, and his wife was a Henderson from Bayhead. (To add to the Bayhead connection, the Macdonalds were friendly with a man who had originally emigrated to Durban but came to the Transvaal for the dry, healthy climate. His name was Donnie MacFarquhar and I knew him as he had moved back to Stornoway when I was a teenager.)

Anyway, the Macdonalds had obviously heard of my presence in the country from another Lewis family whom I used to visit and had mentioned it to the old folks on the farm. Wouldn't it have been even more amazing if it had been me in the glider which had landed on their doorstep! Sadly, I never met the Macdonalds although a visit had been arranged. Mrs Macdonald died suddenly before it could happen. She had started knitting a pullover for me and it was still on the pins.

Mrs Jouber from the grocery shop had a sister called Mrs Mannix. She lived in a very big house which had been a VIP residence in the days before the Union of South Africa. Mrs Mannix had several daughters, all of whom had the names of flowers. I only remember Hyacinth. She worked in a bank and made me open an account. She encouraged me to make a deposit every time I called. When I left the country I had over £100 in my account. I couldn't believe it!

The mother was a big woman who walked with a heavy lurch to one side. She probably needed a hip replacement, but it'll be too late now! Her mother, a Mrs Bissett, lived with them. She was the opposite of her daughter; small and slight, with a mass of white hair. It was hard to imagine her riding bareback, as she told me she used to do, shooting springbok in the head so as not to spoil the meat. Although she was of Afrikaans stock, she married a Scot before the Boer War broke out.

The house had a wide corridor running from the front to the dining room at the other end, with the kitchen behind that. Mrs Bissett had a 'boy' to work in the garden (he was probably in his forties!) who was not allowed into the house to wash his hands; there was a tap in the garden which he was expected to use.

One day there was the sound of a loud commotion and screaming coming from the kitchen, so Mrs Mannix lurched her away along the corridor as fast as she could go. Going through the dining room she saw her old mother, standing wringing her hands. In the kitchen, she saw a battle going on between the garden boy and the kitchen maid. Apparently he had come in to the kitchen to try to wash his hands and the kitchen maid, who knew the rule, had tried to put him out. He had picked up the kitchen knife and was threatening the terrified maid.

Mrs Mannix didn't hesitate. She caught them both by their hair and banged their heads together. They sank to the floor and she quickly disposed of the knife. The boy jumped up, dazed, shook his head and ran off. Being dazed, unfortunately, he made for the wrong door, going towards the front of the house through the dining room with Mrs Mannix in hot pursuit. After she had seen him off the premises, she returned to the kitchen to see to the girl who was none the worse for her experience. There was, however, no sign of her mother. Eventually she appeared, crawling out from under the huge sideboard. It was not clear whether she had been knocked over by the culprit as he ran away, or whether she had hidden there for her own safety!

One incident from my two years stationed in the Transvaal still puzzles me. A South African, whom I didn't know very well, living in a room near mine, asked me to do him a favour. He said he had left his car in a town near where he had been stationed previously. He wanted someone to go with him on our day off duty in a big, posh car he had borrowed from his girlfriend, to collect his own car. His plan was that I would drive his car back and he would come back in the borrowed car. I think now what an idiot I was to agree. I had very little driving experience, no licence, and I don't remember anything about having insurance.

Anyway, off we went for what was to be a whole day's driving, there and back. On the way he told me the name of the car I was to drive. I remember it was a double-barrelled name: Armstrong-Siddely or Oldsmobile 'Something'. (It certainly was old!) He also said it had pre-selecting gears, which didn't mean anything to me. His next piece of information was that the starter didn't work so it would have to be pushed to get it going. There was no starter handle.

Worse was to follow. He told me that the car was in the house belonging to his ex-girlfriend's father. He was the mayor of the town and did not like my friend very much. He suggested that I should go to the door of the house and ask for the key of Flight Sergeant Tomlinson's car. If things went well, an African maid would answer the door; if they didn't, the 'old man' himself would come to the door. "Don't run away if he has a gun," he joked, "in case he thinks you are me!"

Fortunately, it was a maid who answered when I went to the door, while he skulked out of sight. The maid brought the key and we got the car out. Amazingly, it started. He ran the engine for a few minutes and showed me how to work the strange gears. Imparting final advice about stopping on a hill, he got into his new girlfriend's car and off he went. We must have got petrol somewhere, although I can't remember where. I hope the rascal paid for it! For some reason, he indicated that we would travel back by a side road. I was puzzled by this but did not have a chance to inquire as to why.

The first town I went through had traffic lights; my first experience of them. I almost didn't see them and had to stop suddenly. Of course, this caused the engine to stop and soon there was a car behind me blowing its horn. I thought of Hardy saying to Laurel, "That's another fine mess you've got us into!"

There was a group of African youths relaxing in the sun on the stoep (a veranda along the pavement in all country towns in South Africa). They seemed to guess my predicament and gathered around the car to give me a push. What a relief! The engine started! I grabbed the loose change I had in my pocket and threw it to them, hoping they were more than rand coins or pennies.

The next part of my journey was along a very deserted road, for many miles; no traffic and no habitations. The veldt is almost a desert, miles and miles of nothing, but when the rain comes it is transformed, almost like the machair. As I felt I was alone in the word, I opened the car's roof and started singing.

Suddenly, I spied an object I the distance, beside the road. I couldn't make out what it was. It crossed my mind that there were unfriendly animals in that part of the world. I quickly shut the roof in case a lion or leopard was waiting to leap up on the car and eat me at its leisure.

As I got nearer, I realised it was a human figure. Then I saw it was a disabled man, with two walking sticks and arm supports. He lifted one to indicate that he wanted a lift. He had callipers on both legs and was wearing some sort of neck support. My problem was that if I stopped the car to give him a lift and the engine cut out, I could hardly ask this poor soul to push the car. I stopped carefully, managing to keep the engine running. The road here was completely flat: no chance of a free-wheeling start.

The next problem was getting him into the car: he was too stiff to bend and so I had to kind of slide him into the back seat. He didn't seem disposed to talk; in fact, he said very little. Eventually, he said, in English, that there was a road coming up on the right where he wanted to be dropped. I offered to take him further to wherever he was going but he said, "No, this will do."

I felt bad leaving him without any shelter from the sun, not even a tree. But the big mystery that has plagued my mind ever since is, how did he get there, miles from anywhere, no houses and no cars? Had someone taken him out onto the road and dumped him there? Had he said something to annoy someone who had given him a lift? There were strong factions in the country at the time, some of it no doubt stemming from the Boer War. One had to be very careful about what one said. However, it was extremely strange that a severely disabled man, who could barely walk, had been left miles from anywhere, in that heat.

Later, I discovered that my friend with the car was possibly known to the police. He had been a 'dagga' runner. Dagga is a plant, grown and dried by Africans, then smoked. It was illegal but widely used. I had assumed it was like tobacco, but found out eventually that it was more like cannabis. Given that he was involved in transporting it, it is likely that the police would have recognised his car. No wonder he wanted us to travel on the side roads! I was lucky not to have been stopped by the police. I wonder if they would have given me a push if I had stalled?

Another episode from that period of my life happened after I fell asleep on a train one day and went miles past where I was heading. I jumped out at the next stop and headed for the bus station to catch a bus back to where I was going. At the bus stop I met a friendly lady with two daughters, so we chatted while we waited, and again on the bus. When she introduced me to her daughters I got the impression that they weren't interested in a humble sergeant when there were Wing Commanders and the like about.

Their mother was another matter. I told the lady that I was from an island out in the Atlantic. She seemed particularly interested in this information. A little thought came into my head that her interest stemmed from a desire to introduce her daughters to a man with little chance of anything other than white blood in his veins. (Ironically, I often thought that the more swarthy islanders who had been out at the peats for a few days would have had a bit of difficulty getting on the segregated buses in South Africa in these days!) I was cordially invited to come and visit them.

Before the visit could take place, a beautifully hand-knitted pullover came to me by post. It must have been knitted by the mother as the daughters didn't look like hand-knitters to me. The problem of how to respond to this gift was solved for me: a guy in a neighbouring room saw the jersey and asked if he could borrow it to go on a date. He was posted elsewhere and I am still waiting to get it back!

Another recollection that comes into my mind from this time relates to a 'bioran' I had regarding a car. A 'bioran' in my understanding gives the idea of a deep shock or disappointment, following a big build-up of anticipation. By this time I was in the Cape Province and had been told to visit a pair of elderly sisters, one a widow from the First World War and the other unmarried. One had been a physiotherapist. They were family friends from long ago. One had been ill, but got out of bed and came downstairs when I visited. I trimmed the hedge and took the dog for a walk.

They were very nice to me so I visited regularly, doing little jobs for them. The one who had been ill had a bit of a revival because of my visits and regularly ate downstairs. Finally, I took them to the theatre. They must have got the idea that they it would be useful to have me around more permanently. Their plan, if they had captured me, was that I would be given a rondavel (a traditional African thatched house) which had been left to the physiotherapist one by a grateful patient, and a little car. I was mortified to learn that they had gone so far as to phone by Commanding Officer to ask for me to be transferred to an airfield nearer their home.

A short while I heard this, my CO said to me, "Hey, you. Do you know there is a car for you waiting to be collected down at the railway station?"

"What?" I said, nearly fainting. It was about the time of my birthday. "Golly," I thought, "the ladies have decided to give me the car as a birthday present."

"You'd better go and get it," he said.

Off I went to get the bus. My heart was thudding with excitement. I was delighted to think that this would be the last time I waited for that old thing. "A single, please," I said gleefully to the conductor, glancing at the sign which read, 'Verbode om te spu.' I always thought it was a revolting sign, even after I learned some Afrikaans and discovered it meant, 'Forbidden to spit.' Not quite as bad as I thought!

At last, I reached the railway station. I remember the station master's face still, and the glasses down at the end of his nose, as he looked at his paperwork. Meantime, I spied the car in the yard. "What a little beauty," I thought.

"You'd better come and sign for it," said the station master, passing me a list of names. I scanned the list. The only Macfarlane I could see was a Lieutenant Macfarlane. I was only a Sergeant! The car was not for me. It was obviously for a South African posted to our camp from some distance away.

What was to follow was worse. Word had spread in the camp that I was away to pick up a car, so when I came off the bus, faces were appearing at windows and I had to make my way along, trying not to look how I felt. That was a bioran!

Another car-related story relates to my friend, Bert. We travelled together once on a troop ship. On one occasion he was very ill. In the services, you could not just send for a doctor; you had to go 'on sick parade'. This was not always straightforward, but when I went to the medical section I met a doctor who recognised my accent and wanted to speak about 'Steornabhagh mor a' chaisteal'. I was then able to persuade him that my friend was skeletal, and could barely stand. A stretcher was sent for him and he was taken to hospital where he recovered. He had dysentery.

Bert and I bought an old banger for £50. One day were driving it somewhere and had picked up two unsuspecting hitchhikers. There was a clinking noises coming from a back wheel and the car kept stopping. We discovered that the wheel wasn't turning. We were able to limp along for a bit until we met a level crossing. "Will we risk it?" we considered. It was only a small car so we managed to lift the rear end and wheel it across the railway line like a pram! No train came, fortunately.

Eventually we reached a town called Heidelburg where we left in a garage. A 'seized differential' was diagnosed. We had plenty of trouble with that car. I later cut my losses and Bert 'bought me out'.

Bert and I had done up our basic rooms, making them fairly comfortable. Mrs MacAulay, ex Tolsta Chaolais, lived in Jo'burg and made curtains. We had springbok skins on the floor and painted the walls with red stoep paint. As the nights were quite cold, we got a little heater. Our rooms became a favourite gathering place in the evenings.

Bert decided to renovate the car and there were plenty of volunteers to help dismantle it. Unfortunately, they were not so quick to take away all the parts, so our nice rooms were full of these; silencer, wheels and other unmentionables. Bert was then posted to Cape Town, leaving me with all this stuff in my room, and it all belonged to him! Unluckily, the CO made a weekly inspection of the barrack blocks accompanied by a long retinue of minions, including the station warrant officer. He had been in my room when it was immaculate so he confidently guided the CO and his followers in my direction. Alas, when they opened the door, their eyes popped! "Whose room is this?" the CO bawled. "Tell him this is not a garage!"

Every week after that, I had to borrow a wheelbarrow and load all that stuff on to it and hide it until after the inspection was over. Then came a message from Bert. He had sold the car in part exchange for another vehicle in Cape Town. The new owner had been posted to my camp and was due to arrive. "Can you please put it together before he arrives?" asked Bert.

Unfortunately, I was away for the weekend when this message came, and the new owner got there before me. What a rage he was in when he saw the car was in bits! I suppose I could have said that it was nothing to do with me, but I got a grumpy engineer in the room next door to help, and we put it together. There was some small bit left over, but amazingly, after we put some petrol in, it went! I met Bert some years later in England, but I don't think he really appreciated how much he owed the engineer.

A sad story I remember is another example of the strange coincidences which seem to follow me around. One day I was travelling in a train in a seat next to the corridor. I suddenly became aware of banging noises and felt a draught of air. I looked out and saw an RAF man standing facing the open door, with a hand on each side. I rushed out and reached him just as he started to move forward. He didn't struggle, but I held onto him until the guard came along and shut the door. I asked him to find an empty compartment and I stayed with the chap for the rest of the journey. He didn't speak, except to offer me a peppermint. When I declined, he said,

"I certainly cannot. It's a perfectly good night," the grumpy voice continued. "You can walk along the railway track."

"How far is it?" I asked.

"A few miles. Not far." Then he hung up.

My new friend indicated that I could leave my gear in a store and I set off. There must have been villages along the way that I couldn't see, because several times in the course of my walk hundreds of dogs started barking.

In the morning I arrived at the gates of the camp and fell asleep in the guard room.

My posting to Shallufa or El Ganayen had a sad connection. My friend Hamish from Aberdeen had been killed there some time before. We had been walking and chatting somewhere once when he said to me, "One day you'll be saying what a nice guy I was." So, here I am, saying it now, Hamish, to any of the folk we once knew, who are left.

On the other hand, another thing about El Ganayen that made me smile is that 'El Ganayen' in Arabic means 'The Gardens'. I never saw one!

I joined a station near the Bitter Lake. The Suez Canal runs through it. There were quite a number of dinghies and canoes on the lake which were used by personnel who were stationed there in their free time. The system was, I was informed, that a sailing dinghy needed a crew of four. Each person bought a share. If you were posted away your share was returned to you and someone else bought it. It was similar for a canoe although only two shares were required. (I've only just remembered that I never got my share refunded! Too late now!)

I had a quarter share in a sailing dinghy and a half share in a canoe. The person I shared the canoe with hardly spoke. He would just come to see if I was free to go out for a paddle. One day we went off across the lake, in the usual silence, before deciding to pull the canoe up on a spit of sand, for a rest. Near us there were two parallel rows of concrete pillars to guide ships passing through the canal. After a while my companion said, "Fancy a swim across the canal to one of these concrete markers? We can dive off it and swim back. The canal is deep enough there for a dive."

There is a strong force of water flowing through the canal, and it is not tidal. The markers were probably about ten feet high with metal rods fixed to the sides. There were a lot of shells attached to the concrete and, as we climbed up, I cut my toe on one of these. As we rested on top of the pillar, I noticed my toe was bleeding, but it didn't bother me until we dived back into the water and I remembered I had seen a sign saying, 'SHARK WARNING. NO SWIMMIMG.' I remembered that blood attracts sharks, so began to feel panic. Just then, I felt something touch my leg. I kicked out at whatever it was, and was relieved that it appeared to be nothing harmful.

Then I happened to glance along the canal and spotted what I thought was a wisp of smoke in the distance. It seemed quite far off, so I swam on, but when I looked at it again, the wisp of smoke was actually the bow of a large ship. I could see the bow-wave and could hear the vroom vroom of the engine. I really started to panic then as it bore down on me, trying to swim faster, but soon becoming exhausted. I told myself to try to keep calm and breathe deeply. I tried not to look to the right and to concentrate on avoiding the propellers.

My companion had reached the canoe and shouted, "Look out! Hurry up!"

At last, I passed the marker pillar on the other side and reached the canoe. My companion said, "A close one, that," just as a large naval warship went swishing past: HMS *Invincible* (*Incorrigible? Incompatible? Incomparable?* Something like that.)

Another adventure I had on the lake happened one day when, with none of the other 'shareholders' available, I decided to take the dinghy out by myself for the first time. It was fairly easy going out. There was a good breeze and I tacked along, doing quite well and feeling rather pleased with myself. A mistake! After some time, I turned down-wind and jibbed back to the long, low jetty to which all the other boats were moored by the bow, each in its own place.

I turned into my own place, dropped the sail, left the tiller, and went forward to tie up. Unfortunately, when you are sailing on your own you have to be quick to the bow if there is a wind or the boat will slew away from the mooring. Of course, I was not quick enough, and the wind blew the dinghy along to the boat next to it and the bowsprit went right into it. I don't mean a scratch – it went right in, made a hole, and stuck. I was nearly sick. It was the CO's boat!

It was a skin-coated boat so I was able to extract the bowsprit quite easily. Although the skin went back in place, I was not tempted to pretend that nothing had happened. Instead, I went to see him and explained that I made a hole in his boat. He was very forgiving, warned me not to go out in the boat alone again, and said that it would be fixed in the workshop.

I was so grateful that I would have given him a bit of my own skin to patch it with!

Another maritime experience which I have just remembered happened somewhere in the southern hemisphere in a troopship. It is probably something which is quite familiar to real mariners. I happened to look out a porthole and couldn't believe my eyes: the whole ocean had turned into molten silver. It is hard to describe. The water was not just shining; the waves and bow-wave seemed to have the texture and appearance of liquid silver. I ran up on deck. So excited was I that I went up the ladder to the deck reserved for senior officers. Lights were completely forbidden in that area so I thought none of the eminent people would be able to spot that I was an inferior being.

The vision that I saw was caused by the presence of phosphorous in the water and the complete dark of the night. The only similar experience I had had was when I was very young, long before light switches or refrigeration. I opened a cupboard door where a plate of fish was sitting, ready for cooking. In the pitch darkness, it was transformed into a mound of strange, eerie light, like a cold fire, or diamonds. Obviously, the fish had been caught where there had been a quantity of phosphorous in the water. I don't know how frequently this happens, but the complete darkness required is difficult to find nowadays.

I did see a mirage once in Egypt, but I cannot remember the explanation. Flying fish was another phenomenon that was interesting to see. Knowing that their 'wings' were actually fins did not detract from the strangeness of the sight.

As I said earlier, coincidences and strange meetings were a feature of my war-time experience. I was in a transit camp waiting to me transported back home at the end of the war. The camp was so big that it would have taken a long time to get from one part of it to another on foot. One daily trip that everybody made was to look at the lists posted up of the names of the next batch to be shipped back home. Fortunately they had a 'gharrie' or lorry going round continually like a bus. It was open to the air and standing room only.

I jumped on to it one day. It was packed and, as we wobbled along, I heard my name coming out of the crowd. A figure shoved its way through and I was greeted with a warm handshake. He was amazed to see me and keen to find out where I had been stationed. He obviously knew me quite well from somewhere but I could not place him. When I got off the bus he said, "Where's your billet? I'll call for you for a swim."

I told him and he and his pals called for me every day to swim and sunbathe. His pals called him 'Dusty'. He never said anything that gave me an inkling of who he was. This went on for a week or two, when he suddenly said, "You don't know who I am, do you?"

"How did you know?" I asked.

"Because you have never asked about my mother and father. Or Nan."

Of course it all became clear then. I was so embarrassed. I had been in his house and had been out ice-skating with his sister Nan. I realised then where his nickname 'Dusty' came from – his surname was Miller, and all Millers were nicknamed Dusty in the services. Theirs was the house I had visited where the Sgiathanach had been billeted; the fellow I had met in the south of England and, briefly, in an African jungle.

Dusty, or Sandy, told me of an even more amazing coincidence he had been involved in when he was posted to Kenya. He had just arrived in Nairobi and was spoken to by a man who, recognising his white knees, said "Just arrived?" The man told Sandy that he was married to a Scottish nurse and invited him to come to their farm to meet her.

So off they went. On meeting Sandy, the lady asked, "Where are you from?"

"Aberdeen," replied Sandy.

"So am I," replied the nurse. "Which part?"

"Hilton, such-and-such street," said Sandy.

There was dead silence for a few seconds. Then the howling started. He was her little brother whom she hadn't seen for sixteen years. She had been nursing abroad and married a patient and they now worked on their own farm. They had been struggling for some years until the war came. A weed-like plant, which had no value, grew on their farm. It was discovered that it was in demand as a dressing for war wounds. They were now doing very well as a result of this.

It was another strange war time story.

Pat in his RAF uniform at
the beginning of the war

At a wedding, after the war

"Yes, I would say so."

"So, you're not sure?

"As far as I can see, it looks exactly the same."

"So, you're not sure?"

"How can anyone be 100% sure?"

"May I remind you that I am the one asking the questions?"

And so on. It was like a game.

The Sheriff was also a bit of a wit. He said to one of the accused, "So, you opened this wagon, or as you say, you found it open. Did you think you had found Aladdin's Cave?"

As the trial drew to a close, the verdict was 'Guilty as charged'. The Sheriff announced there would be a break for lunch before sentencing. Dowdall requested, "Your Honour, the accused X, has requested that he be allowed time to get married during the lunch break."

The Sheriff removed his glasses, the way they do, and said, "I don't see any reason why not. Very well."

We guessed that this was Dowdall trying to get some sympathy, possibly to reduce the sentence.

When we reassembled, His Honour announced, "Mr X, you have been found guilty of a serious charge. I'm afraid you will have to wait some time for your honeymoon. You will go to prison for three years. Take him down."

The buying and shipping of tweed from the 'small producers' went on for some time. Market conditions made it what is called a 'sellers' market' as the shortage of products put the sellers in an advantageous position. Quite suddenly, however, everything changed to a buyers' market. Supplies became more plentiful and buyers could be particular about designs and process. This meant that a lot of the 'small producers' gave up producing and looked about for buyers of remaining stocks.

Some of the more successful of their number had quite considerable stocks and I was approached by at least four that I can remember whom I had never bought from before. I was able to arrange sales to 'my' factory in England. Fortunately the transactions were successful. One of them told me years later that what I did just about saved him from a divorce! When I handed over a large cheque to another, he started trying to hand over a wad of £20 notes. Although I could probably have done with the money, I refused to accept it as I was already paid as an agent.

"Take it as a wedding present," he said. "I hear you are getting married."

He had mixed me up with someone else!

So that was the end of that phase in my life and I was quite relieved. I had never seen the man from the court case again until the other day and it brought back a lot of memories.

I then became involved in the development of hand knitting. A mainland mill developed a yarn that was similar to Harris yarn but softer for use. Patterns were produced for the local knitters, of whom we seemed to employ hundreds. We were eventually producing a nice garment in several different designs and colours. The designs were traditional and slightly similar to those produced in the Irish Aran Islands. We made the mistake of using agents who were always keen to get big orders. Unfortunately, as soon as the spring came the hand-knitting ladies downed tools; delivery dates and penalty clauses were of no interest to them. All very stressful for me!

I'm also amazed that I survived all the encounters I had with the sharks I came across in the business world. We supplied some shops on the east coast of the United States as well as in France, England and in mainland Scotland. We only once sent an order to Japan because they insisted it be sent expensively in a wooden crate. I had a subsequent visit from a young man from South Lochs who told me he was First Officer on a merchant ship sailing to the East. One of his duties was checking the cargo being slung aboard. To his amazement, he saw this crate with 'Loch Erisort' (our trade name) on it! I was able to tell him that the box probably contained jerseys knitted by his mother who was one of our knitters.

One of the predicaments I got myself into at this time didn't happen in Stornoway but involved 'locals'. A lady friend had married an

Englishman and had gone with him to various places as the job required. At this time they were in a big flat in Glasgow. She missed home and her old pals, so when any acquaintances were in the city she expected them to call or to stay. On this particular occasion, to save her trouble, I had booked into the Royal Stewart Hotel and asked the couple to join me for a meal. Incidentally, I was very impressed with the automatic doors in this hotel. I had never come across the likes before!

My friend's husband could not come as he was due on night shift so she came by herself. Perhaps it was just as well as he might have been a bit bored by the Stornoway stories! After dinner, we were sitting in the lounge, chatting. There was only one other group there, so it was very quiet when suddenly the door crashed open and a person staggered in. There are various words to describe how his condition: 'maroculous', 'well oiled', 'plastered', 'palutered', any of them would do. I thought to myself, "Thank goodness, he's no-one we know."

But, when he spied us and lurched over, I realised he was a 'local' and he knew my companion.

"We called round to see you and your husband said you were out with HIM," he said to her, glaring at me. Just then, his wife appeared, clutching her handbag nervously. I offered them something to eat but he wasn't interested in eating. I could hardly believe it when he staggered over and got a cheque cashed at the bar. He went off in search of liquid and his wife told us the story. He had been a painter and decorator to trade but had lost his job 'through the drink'. She hissed, "We had to sell our flat. I have the remains of the money in my handbag. He's got another job now as an undertaker. (I had noticed the pin-striped trousers, now she mentioned it.) It has its own accommodation but we'll have lost it now," she added, "because he got drunk at a funeral today."

Before he returned with a bottle, she asked me to try to get his car keys off him and drive them home. I was most reluctant as I was not used to city driving and much preferred travelling in taxis. I had, in fact, ordered a taxi for myself and my friend, so when it arrived the two ladies got into it. I told the taxi driver the story and he said I could follow him. The palutered undertaker, gurgling whisky down his throat like a drain, straight from the bottle, threw me the keys of his vehicle. "Here, you can drive," he said. He led me along Clyde Street, not to a car, but to a HEARSE!

"I can't drive this," I thought, taking in the length and the tinted-glass windows. "I can't see behind me properly." But I could see the taxi waiting, so I just shut my eyes, hoped for the best and reversed out into the traffic. It was a flat-fronted vehicle with the engine in the cab and a sliding door which I couldn't manage to shut. "Have a swig!" my passenger kept shouting.

I soon lost sight of the taxi and the undertaker's directions were somewhat confused. What made the journey even worse was that every time I speeded up the door slid open and when I slowed down it shut. When we reached my friends' home, I was sweating and my knees were shaking. I was relieved as I thought my ordeal was over. But, no, we still had to get to the undertaker's flat. His wife climbed in, followed by my friend, who wanted to make sure I did not get into any trouble.

"I can't drive like this," I protested it. "I'm too squashed and the door won't stay shut. I could land on the road when we go round a corner."

The undertaker rather grudgingly offered to move into the back of the hearse, where he lay back, almost comatose, but still clutching the bottle. I stopped at lights where a policeman was standing. He waved us through, saluting respectfully. Maybe he thought there were remains in the back of the hearse. Little did he know it was a dead drunk!

We eventually arrived at our destination and my friend and I were invited in. It was a funeral parlour, with rows of seats, shelves with top hats, and other necessities. The wife disappeared, possibly to hide the money, and we were offered a swig from the bottle. When we declined, our host said rather sneeringly, "Oh, I see. You want glasses?" When he went off to get some we made our escape.

Some years later I saw him in Stornoway, looking fit and prosperous. He was a widower by then and was in the habit of taking holidays abroad. Indeed, he had a Moroccan lady on his arm! People are amused to hear of that experience, but it was far from funny at the time.

If one is blessed, or cursed, with a good memory there are maybe thousands of events and experiences which can come to mind for no easily explained reason. Some, like the undertaker story, can be funny, others are tragic, and some raise a smile. One such involves two unexpected visitors with connections to the house next door. Before the First World War, a little boy lived next door. When he was a toddler, he formed a bond with my mother who used to play games with him. During the War, after she got married, my father was home on leave from France and 'a knock came to the door'. My father opened it and the little boy asked, "Is Katie Ellen coming out to play?"

Moving on more than fifty years to a dark evening when the hall light had 'refused' (as an elderly lady nearby used to say when a bulb blew), the whole family was temporarily staying at No. 16. Another 'knock came to the door'. A middle-aged man was there, surrounded by luggage; two huge suitcases and other bags. The darkness of the hall and the evening meant I could not identify him at all. He introduced himself as Calum Macdonald, son of Annie Macrae from next door. He was none other than the little boy who had played with my mother. I brought him in, with all his luggage, and went up the street to find my mother who was visiting a friend. I left him at the mercy of our friend, Murdo Tully, who would have made a good inquisitor.

My mother could hardly believe that her old friend had returned. She would have liked to put him up in the house but it was full so, after an evening of catching up, we took him to the Royal Hotel. He stayed there until a relative, who had a B & B, took him in. With some encouragement from her, he eventually moved back to Canada where he had some remaining family.

It was strange to think that, although there had been no communication with him over the half century since he left Stornoway, he expected to find these two houses still there and his old friend too. I'm glad he found both, although his friend was, by then, well into her eighties. After he went back to Canada letters began arriving, one of which in particular continues to cause amusement in the family with its mixture of bad news ('Johnny passed away in October. He would be alive today only for a party making him drink Canadian whisky at his age, 88 or 89'), medical conditions ('Annie Mary's husband was in hospital getting his eyes fixed. Hair was growing under the lids') and his own exploits ('I was struck by lightning last March. It went into my left ear and went through to my right. It left a scab on my nose'). The briefness of the letter is explained in a scribbled note, in pencil: 'Excuse short note. The pen won't write.'

One morning, a few years later, yet another knock at the door revealed a young backpacker who said that his granny had lived next door, making him a nephew of our previous visitor. I took him in, gave him refreshments and went to warn my mother. She came down to speak to him. He introduced himself as Ron, but we did not catch his surname. He went out to look for accommodation, but my mother wanted him to stay given her old friendship with the family. That left me on the sofa again, and trying to combine looking after our guest with going to work.

He obviously intended to stay for good, as he went to the Jobcentre to look for work However, as he did not get a job he eventually left to continue his 'grand tour' of Europe.

Some years later, I got a letter from Ron, saying he was coming for another visit but that this time he would be bringing a North American Indian. When I went down to meet the ferry, I saw one passenger whom I thought might have been a 'Red Indian' (as we used to say when we watched them in Will Mack's Picture House), but no sign of Ron. I returned to the house where the phone rang shortly after. It was Ron phoning to say that he had missed me at the ferry.

"Where's the Indian?" I asked.

"He didn't get a visa," he replied, mysteriously.

So, I went back down to collect him and saw that he had changed since his last visit: his clothes were 'home made' out of deerskins, and his hair was braided, emphasising his high cheekbones. He wore moccasins and his complexion was darker. I realised that he was the Native American. He had been working as a social worker in the Northern Territories and this was where his clothes had been made. They had obviously been home-cured and smelt not unlike a kipper shed.

One evening he was waiting for me in the shop before going home for our evening meal. A customer alerted me to a burning smell, but it was

take off his shoes at the door. I don't know how he disposed of her! I was, however, a little suspicious of his current wife: she wore knee-high leather boots that made me think of a storm-trooper's jack boots, and was fairly bossy herself. Once, when I was passing their open door, I saw him standing on a chair, with his pipe in one hand and a wallpaper scraper in the other. When I suggested that this wall was taking quite a time, he winked and said, "I'm making it last!"

The lady had two little dogs. I asked her what breed they were and she called them 'Foxtrot terriers' rather than 'fox terriers'. Perhaps I should have corrected her, but it was quite a funny error. She then told me that she was the President of the Munich Dog Club. Their Annual General Meeting followed by a meal and social evening was coming up and she invited me to attend with her and her husband. He was to provide the music with an old wind-up gramophone and records. It was the time of the October Beer Festival and she had booked part of the Bier Garten for the occasion. She took me with her to help decorate it, which was pretty difficult as I could not make her out easily because of her Bavarian accent. She gave me a bag of raw potatoes and a box of Dog Club flags. I had to stick each flag in a potato and put one on every table.

My hostess suggested I go off for a walk while the business part of the meeting was on as it would be rather boring for me. That was fine, but when I got back I realised that all the members had brought their dogs with them to the meeting! I could hardly believe it – the noise was tremendous. Then the waiters started bringing in the food and, of course, big steins (jugs) of beer. The latter were so full that a lot spilt on the floor and the dogs lapped it up. This seemed to make them more aggressive, especially when the owners started dropping tit-bits for them. After a brief spell of sleeping, they woke up when my neighbour started playing his wind-up gramophone. What howling that produced!

This was supposed to be a signal for the dancing to start. The Bavarian husbands sat with their noses almost in their beers, looking bored. I thought it was a shame after my neighbour bringing his gramophone, so suddenly I found myself bowing to a lady who jumped up like a shot. I had suggested a waltz to my friend, the music man, so my partner and I swirled around to the 'Blue Danube'.

The husbands continued to sit and scowl until my neighbour shouted out that the only man dancing was a foreigner. This seemed to make them get up and take to the floor. I don't know if my performance that night did any good for international relations!

At one point in the evening a school girl was taken against her will to sit with me because she was learning English at school. To try to make conversation with her I asked her what had been on the Agenda of the meeting. "They are talking about making a trip to Paris," she replied, seriously.

I asked her if the trip was for the humans and the dogs or just the humans. We agreed that there could be problems if all the dogs had to travel by train in the guard's van for 400 miles!

While I was in Munich, my neighbours had a visit from their son who lived in Canada and his Canadian wife. They took them out for a meal one night and invited me and a retired teacher from the flat above. When she arrived I was struck by her similarity to another retired teacher who lived in a flat in New Street in Stornoway. "Are you sure your name is not Cathody Matheson?" I said. I told her about her double who owned a little car but never learnt to reverse. She would have passed her test many years ago when standards were not so strict. Once, on her way to school, she took the wrong turning and found herself on the wrong road. She had to go all the way to Barvas to turn!

All the little domestic touches (putting out the bins; going to the grocers and butchers; going to church; going for meals and to concerts) reminded me that this was the reality of life here, and that putting on uniforms and trying to kill each other was wrong.

Another man I met at this time could not speak any English and asked me (in German) why I was trying to learn his language. When I explained that I liked to be able to speak to the many German tourists I met in my line of business, he looked at me in mock astonishment and said, "I thought Churchill won the war!" As he was leaving, he turned at the door and quoted, "My heart's in the Highlands, my heart is not here; my heart's in the Highlands, a-chasing the deer."

He probably learnt it in school and associated it with Scotland. Touches of humour like that are important in developing good relationships between people and governments.

I was very favourably impressed by all the people I met. A young man even ran after me with my wallet which I left on a shop counter. I enjoyed the language course too. It was funny sitting in a classroom voluntarily. There was even an interval, although I was used to calling it playtime!

Back to Stornoway, and a family story that crops up from time to time is about another animal problem I got involved in once. It was a particularly cold Eastertime and a friend, who lived just outside the town, suggested I bring my young nieces to her house as a setting of ducks was hatching that day.

She had used a broody bantam hen as a surrogate mother, but the hen was really too small to keep all the emerging ducklings under her wings and was getting very nervous. She had chucked two unhatched eggs out of the nest and they were becoming icy cold. I picked them up and could tell that there were ducklings inside. Remembering my early experiences of hens and chickens, I knew that there was a chance they might revive and hatch if they were warmed.

"Well," said my friend, "you can take one of these eggs home and if it hatches you can keep it." I wasn't sure about this, but took it to the nieces' house where we put it in front of the fire. Lo and behold, it started chirping. After a lot of struggling, and to the excitement of the nieces, a little creature stepped out of the shell. Soon it had dried off and was looking round for something to eat. There was a problem with it staying at Anderson Road - the cat was showing too much interest in the duckling, licking its lips and thinking it was Christmas rather than Easter.

So I took it away in a small box. Now, apparently the first thing that a duckling sees it takes to be its mother. So I had to perform the function and dip its beak in water the way its mother would have done to teach it to drink. Another thing I remembered from having chickens and hens was the low, sad , whistling sound a chick would make if it was separated from its mother. The mother would respond by making a special little clucking sound and the chick would rush to it. I soon discovered that ducklings do just the same! Every time I went into the kitchen, I would hear the low, sad whistle, and every time I came back into the living room it started quivering its little wings with delight, and climbing onto my foot!

At one o'clock in the morning, I was wondering what to do with a newly hatched duckling which clearly thought I was its parent. When I went to bed I put it back in its box on top of the radiator to keep it warm. The whistling noise continued throughout the night. What a welcome I got in the morning!

Sadly, this 'foster placement' could not last as I had a shop to run, so it was repatriated to Sandwick.

Thinking of my shop-keeping days, probably 40 years ago, reminds me what a lot of work was involved: looking for stock, doing window displays, preparing accounts, repairs and maintenance, and many more activities. The work I like best to remember is the twice-yearly visits to Trade Fairs around the country. The ones we visited were usually in Aviemore, Ingliston, Dublin and Harrogate. I found them interesting and enjoyable, although hard work. We built up a good relationship over the years with certain exhibitors, so meeting them every year made it a social occasion, too.

Going round the stalls all day, for three days, could be quite exhausting. I always took one of the ladies from the shop away; each got a turn. They were brilliant at looking after tickets and bookings, and even driving my car when I took it. They were good drivers so I could relax!

Sometimes they were exhausted after a long day on their feet, looking at all the goods on display, making decisions, talking and listening, and all they needed was a meal and an early night. Not Maggie! With social events in the evening, she would be dancing as long as there was a peep of music coming from the band, and of course I was forced to follow suit...I remember one occasion when the dances were all Scottish and we were definitely the best at the reels and Strathspeys.

On another occasion at a Trade Fair in Dublin, my companion and I arrived in the huge building where the event was happening. She spotted the sign for the toilets and decided to go before we started work. We arranged that I would stay there until she returned as neither of us was familiar with the building. Well, I waited, and waited, and waited. I don't know how long she was away, but it seemed a VERY long time. I was beginning to think that she had been abducted when she eventually reappeared, looking rather agitated. She had been locked in the toilet!

On my Munich trip, I had to look after my passport, money, tickets and bookings, and really missed the efficiency of the girls from the shop. On my return from Bavaria, I managed to book myself on two different trains going to the Channel port. When I set off on the correct train, I found my compartment with the usual passenger list displayed outside. My name was there, with the window seat I had requested, but there were two young Germans occupying the window seats, playing cards. They obviously knew one of the seats was mine and did not look happy at prospect of having to move in the middle of the game. I thought to myself, "If I make a fuss and claim this seat, I could start World War Three!"

At the same time, a young Belgian man arrived and claimed his seat. Then he started making a fuss because he could see that I had been done out of the window seat, saying, "Das ist his sitz!" (That is his seat!) and pointing at the seat in question.

I said, trying out my German, "Es macht nicht. Ich sitz heer." ("It doesn't matter. I'll sit here.") I think he was disappointed as he wanted an argument!

Then the train stopped at a station and a gang of loud, noisy youths erupted out of one of those tunnels that sometimes connect stations to platforms. They were full of high spirits and appeared to be football fans. The Belgian watched them with some distaste and I could tell he was ticking them off. In amongst the German words, I heard him refer to the Englisch schweinhunde who would sort them out and realised he was threatening them with me! I kept pretty quiet after that. I finally reached the Channel without further incident, apart from banging my nose on a glass door that I thought was open – it was too clean!

When I reached Edinburgh, I had arranged to visit a Trade Fair at Ingliston, where I spent the day. At closing time I enquired about a bus back in to the city and was told to get 'the green bus from Glasgow'. This gave me problems because I have a colour deficiency and couldn't tell a green Glasgow bus from a red Glasgow bus. I had just decided to get a taxi when I spied a friend going to her car. Muriel offered me a lift and we set off for the town. The next problem was that I could not remember the name of the hotel I was staying in. Fortunately, my brain began working and we were able to piece together which hotel it was when I remembered that it was near the King's Theatre where Calum Kennedy was appearing.

It is worth saying a bit more about my friend, Muriel Macintyre. She was a colourful personality whose pottery we sold in the shop. We never needed to place an order; whenever she had enough for a consignment, she filled her van and came across the Minch to us and we bought it all. It was beautiful and it always sold out.

On one of our visits to Stornoway she spoke about Garrabost clay which had been used by ancient people to make cooking and storage pots; remains of these pots have occasionally been found. In more recent times it had been used to make bricks. We decided to go off down to Garrabost to have a look. When we reached the site, we discovered that it had not been maintained and was full of water-filled pot-holes following a lot of rain. I drove the car slowly through the water before coming to one that was not a shallow puddle. The front wheels sank down into the water, leaving the chassis sitting on the ground.

I left the elegant Muriel sitting in the car, with the water coming in round her feet, to go off in search of someone with a tractor to try to rescue us. There were very few houses around. At one, I was told, "My husband has a heart condition and is not going to push any car." When I asked about a phone, she said there was a public phone across the road which I could use, before shutting the door in my face.

I crossed the road and tried to phone my usual garage but there seemed to be no-one there because it was lunchtime, so I wondered what to do next. Suddenly, I saw several figures surrounding the car, all dressed in white. Next, I saw the car moving backwards and being pushed round to point back the way we had come. Back down I went to find Muriel still in the car. "Who on earth were these people?" I asked.

Her story was that, after I went away to phone, she went exploring and found a building, obviously made of Garrabost brick! Inside there was a number of young men dressed in toe-length white aprons and trousers. They were the Campbell family and their employees from their butchers' business. Muriel had explained her predicament (she could be so charming) and asked if they could do anything to help a damsel in distress. Anyway, they managed to get it out and turn it round, and I drove back to the town.

On another occasion, she asked me to meet herself and a prospective daughter-in-law at the ferry. She was easily recognisable in a cloak and big hat at the top of the gangway. When she reached the pier, she ran over to me and launched herself at me, arms round my neck – I nearly fell backwards. "Oh, darling, I'm so happy to see you!" she screamed. All eyes were on us. This was pure play acting on her part and she enjoyed my embarrassment. She was one of the many memorable characters I met during my shop-keeping years and I was very sorry to hear of her recent death.

The Garrabost clay incident reminds me of another archaeological incident I was involved in. Out for a walk on the machair in Barvas one Sunday afternoon, I was idly looking at some round stones stuck in the sand when I stopped and said to my friend, "That looks like the fissure on top of a human skull."

"Nah," he said, "it's only a stone." But when I smoothed away some sand, there, indeed, was a skull! In my youth, when strapped for cash, I had thoughts of buried treasure and daydreams about finding such riches. By this time, money had become a boring set of figures, some black and some red. But this was still a dream come true! Somehow, I knew that this was the scene of an ancient burial. I carefully parted some surface sand and realised that a whole skeleton was there. I covered the skeleton as deeply as possible for protection from the nearby cows which were wandering about. The skull, however, had been dislodged and was more liable to be damaged, so I decided to take it home for the weekend until I could contact the appropriate authorities.

Professor Harding of the Archaeology Department at Edinburgh University happened to be here on another site with a group of students so I took him to the site. Another expert, Trevor Cowie flew up and engaged a local lady, Margaret Ponting, with experience of archaeology and myself to help with the exposure and some digging. This took a month, and in the meantime I came across two more similar burials, also in the crouched position and with what is called grave furniture, mostly decorated pots. All of this indicated the period from which the bodies came.

The archaeologists said it wasn't fair for a layman to find all these objects when others can be real students for years without finding anything. I was lucky. When the students from the other site were finished, they came over to work on 'my' finds and I was relegated to the task of taking the 'spoil' (dug up sand) in bags to the river in a Land Rover to be sieved and any small objects ticketed. I didn't let on that I had never driven a Land Rover in my life, and the area was very bumpy. However, I managed somehow.

We all came back to the 'dig' the following year, in a wet September. As a result of our efforts, we uncovered the scattered foundations of a structure, or structures, at a lower level than the burials, so pre-dating them in antiquity. There was the usual 'midden' materials round them; mostly shells – what a lot of winkles they ate four thousand years ago! There was the skeleton of a small dog among the stones. We'll never know if a huge storm caused a collapse, perhaps trapping the dog. The structures were just ruins, and probably those who carried out the burials were unaware that there were remains of an ancient structure in the area.

There is little evidence of similar settlements from this era elsewhere in the Western Isles. Maybe they were 'strangers'!

If you look at those bones and say, "It was a late teenage female," it does not evoke any human emotion. If, instead, you say, "She was a teenage girl," and you find a comb made of bone in the area, you feel a twinge of sympathy. You wonder what life was like for her, and how she died.

One final connection: in the last remaining shed of my grandfather's efforts at the back of this house, there is now a pottery in which hundreds of ethnic figures engaged in familiar occupations have been made. It started as a hobby and has, perhaps, represented my last change of occupation. I am really supposed to be working there at present, but I have been struck by a bout of an illness called laziness! There is a garden here too which demands a lot of my attention. I don't think my grandfather would have approved of that!

Pat collecting seaweed for gardening in Barra (1999)

The pottery, 16 Scotland Street

Pat (right) with a visitor

Pat with his grand nephew, Andrew MacDonald

The garden at 16 Scotland Street at it's best

Gardening has been one of pat's favourite pastimes for many years

Pat working on a bust in pottery shed, early 1980s

Bust of Duncan Morrison, 'Major' (now in Taigh Dhonnachadh)

Loch Erisort Woollens, Cromwell Street, 1971

Pat (left) with Iain MacIver, his business partner for many years

The archaeological find at Barvas